Len Gibson with banjo,
Huyton, near Liverpool.
Resting between air raids.

DEDICATION

To my loving wife Ruby. We met in 1945 when she was a nurse and I was a patient, and she has cared for me ever since. To my dear departed mother who treasured and preserved everything I ever wrote. To my father who taught me patience and industry and to my sisters who loved and supported me.

Finally, to all my comrades who were unfortunate enough to be incarcerated in Japanese Prisoner of War Camps.

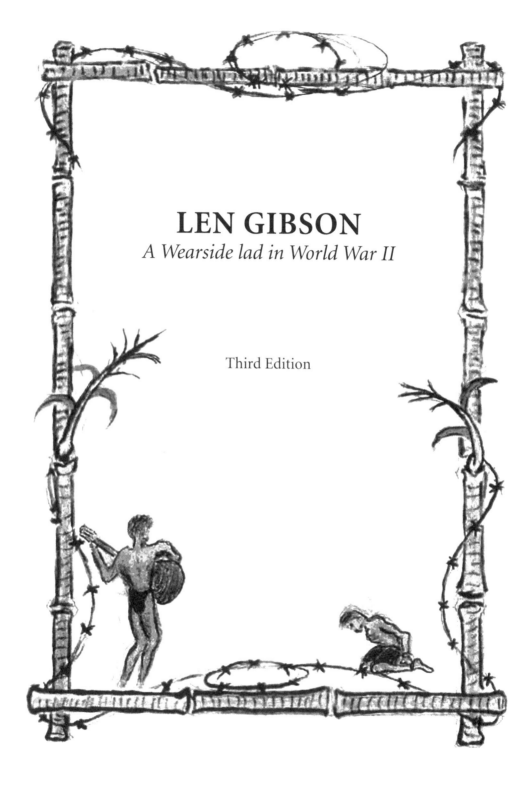

LEN GIBSON

A Wearside lad in World War II

Third Edition

ACKNOWLEDGEMENTS

For contributions to the previous editions: Clinton Leeks OBE, Sheila and David Stewart, John Davison, Derek McInally and Professor Gordon Batho.

Image permissions from North News and Pictures, Sunderland Echo and Northern Echo Newspapers.

To Brian Burnie, founder of the charity Daft as a Brush Cancer Patient Care for financing and initiating this 3rd edition and to Potts Print (UK) for their contributions.

LEN GIBSON
A Wearside lad in World War II

Published by Potts Print (UK) Limited, Northumberland NE23 1WG
© 2021
ISBN 978-0-9927712-5-6

CONTENTS

INTRODUCTION

Dave Stewart - Musician and Co-Founder of the 'Eurythmics'

"At the age of nine my family moved from Barnard Street to Ettrick Grove and only one house away from the Gibson family. We were the last house before the shops, and in the other direction the road curved around the corner so out of our back window we could look over to the Gibson's house. David (son of the family) was very friendly, even setting up a walkie-talkie system to me and my brother's bedroom at one point which was very exciting.

As I was growing up I would often visit the Gibson's even though I was quite a few years younger than David: I was an inquisitive kid, interested and intrigued with everything and everyone around me. At this point I wasn't interested in music at all, but after a few years passed, my brother John and David Gibson both were getting into music, playing guitars and banjos - folk music mainly. However, around the age of ten, I was drawn towards Mr. Gibson (Len) as he had an aura around him and although he was very soft spoken, I loved the sound of his voice and the way he explained things. One day I was at their house and Len picked up a guitar and played it in a magical way: a certain kind of rhythm I'd never heard before and he sang some songs I didn't know. On reflection it seemed to be a mixture of calypso and another influence I still can't put my finger on, but at the time it was like an epiphany."

Image courtesy of Dave Stewart.

Len Gibson with his son David.

My cousin had sent some Blues records from Memphis and David was playing a twelve-string guitar and my brother was always practising with a folk group in the back garden. I was surrounded by music, yet I wasn't making any: I was obsessed with playing football and convinced I would play for Sunderland one day (like every kid in Sunderland!). Then, I had to have a knee operation because of an accident on the football pitch and I was stuck at home recuperating.

Being around the corner to Mr. Gibson and injuring my knee turned out to be very fortuitous - in fact, life changing. I now became interested in how to play guitar and would hobble around to see Mr. Gibson and ask him to play something on guitar so I could see his fingers move on the fretboard and watch his other hand strumming. He didn't sound like the boys in the back garden, he sounded like he was playing the Blues, but he wasn't playing Blues songs: blues is a feeling, and that's why I was so drawn to the sound he was making. To this day I'm in love with the Blues and made a documentary movie in 1992 in Memphis and North Mississippi called 'Deep Blues'.

After everything Mr. Gibson had been through and the fact music kept him and others alive pouring a sense of hope into a seemingly hopeless situation, is a mind-blowing feat of strength and to this day almost impossible for me to comprehend. Len Gibson's way of playing and singing through adversity is an example I have followed ever since I learned to write songs. I cannot explain how much Len and David's enthusiasm for life and music has influenced me on my path, but I am full of gratitude and those moments hearing music played in the Gibson's front room I will never forget.

Dave Stewart
5th March, 2021

FOREWORD

By G F Kershaw (Author of 'Tracks of Death')

For many years I have held the conviction that the book that fully describes the disaster and horror of war has never been and never will be written. As with climbing Everest, only the actual experience gives full understanding.

For example, I remember London burning throughout its vast area following the Battle of Britain; standing on the deck of an overcrowded 26,000-ton troopship in the North Atlantic in January 1941, its engines silent and no-one speaking, awaiting the torpedo that thank God never came; and being within 100 yards of the Kwai Bridge in December 1944 while a squadron of hedge hopping, unchallenged B29's emptied their bomb bays on us. Such things are beyond the capacity of man to portray in words or pictures, or of the inexperienced to understand.

If such experiences are to be withstood, healthy minds and bodies are the best foundations for possible survival. Where Far East captivity was involved, an arrogant and brutal captor had decided, from day one, no such foundations would be permitted. Remember that those who survived three-and-a-half years of captivity had eaten about 4,000 meals of broken rice, all of it infested with maggots, weevils, rat's droppings and urine, and occasionally sawdust, glass and other foreign bodies from the godown floors. Even the impoverished coolies refused to eat it or feed it to their pigs. The rice was occasionally supplemented by pumpkin, fragments of meat and green peas.

Starvation and disease are easy companions, and in the Orient this means dysentery, cholera, malaria, tropical ulcers, diphtheria, hookworm and cirrhosis of the liver. Everyone suffered from beri-beri due to a vitamin deficient diet. Add to this the accidents involved in building the Burma-Siam Railway, the savagery of the guards, the brutality of the Secret Police and the exhausting physical labour through mountainous territory over a period of 16 months, and the final tally of 30,000 deaths can easily be understood.

Despite the vast quantities of drugs and equipment stored in many places by the British authorities in anticipation of a lengthy siege, the Japanese refused to issue them to their captives. As a result, thousands died who could have been saved by medical and surgical intervention. So sudden was the termination of the F E War, due to the bombing of Hiroshima and Nagasaki, that those supplies remained intact in August 1945.

Our captors no longer needed them for themselves.

Come disease, starvation, exhaustion and bombing by one's allies, I think that most FEPOWs would agree that the worst suffering throughout captivity lay in the almost total lack of contact with one's family. Rumours abounded of devastation in the UK through bombing, invasion, etc. and those were enthusiastically amplified by our captors. The few cards that the Japanese allowed us to receive were usually two years old.

Len Gibson's account is a modest record of what is now accepted as one of the greatest disasters of World War II, subjectively and objectively emphasised by understatement and largely left to a compassionate imagination.

A percipient student will also identify the Christian faith by which Len illuminated the darkness for himself and others and the gratitude with which he welcomed his hard-won freedom.

G F Kershaw

George Kershaw was a South Shields lad who, as a conscript, was sent to the Far East in January 1941. He was taken prisoner at the fall of Singapore and worked on the infamous Railway of Death, and later on the more infamous Mergui Road where he met and worked with Len Gibson. He also kept a secret diary.

After returning to England, he worked in local government health and for the NHS – the final twenty-nine years as District Records Medical Officer to North West Durham. He was a fellow of the Association of Medical Records Officers and between 1963 – 74, was Assistant Editor of the Association's journal. When he died in 2004, he was President of the Yasume Far East POW Club.

A Wearside Lad

I was born in Sunderland on 3 January 1920. Our humble home faced onto the wall of a mineral line behind which was the Wagon Way where coal trucks rattled on their journey to the Staithes. Two hundred yards downhill was the entrance to a large shipyard so I was inured to the clamour of shunting trucks, the hammering of rivets into steel, the hooting of ships and tugs. Indeed, all the clamour of a busy riverside.

I was part of a happy and loving family. My father was a conscientious worker who had been blind for most of his early life. An only child, he had had little education and probably never read a book in his whole life. My mother was from a large family; she was very God-fearing and taught my three sisters and I to say our prayers. Sadly, she was rather deaf as a result of the work she did in a munitions factory during World War II.

I attended Bishopwearmouth C of E School until the age of 11 when I passed to attend West Park Central School.

I became a chorister at Bishopwearmouth Church and was for many years the senior boy and soloist.

I left school in 1935 during a depression. Work was hard to find and I had to be content to go and work next to my father in the timber factory. My ambition was to be a teacher and I was determined to further my education by attending night classes.

Len Gibson, 1923 – Aged 3 years.

CHAPTER 1

Your Country Needs You

Early 1939

I was attending Sunderland Technical College doing the London Matric Course: this involved four nights per week studying Science, Maths, English and French. As I was also working full-time at Binn's Factory from 8 until 5 and was also still a member of the church choir, I did not have much spare time. I did, however, manage to go to the cinema one night and one short propaganda film had a message which got through to me. The film was entitled 'The Gap' and it told the story of how, because of a shortage of volunteers, the enemy planes penetrated our defences and bombed our cities.

I was resolved to join a volunteer force. Shortly after this an Army Officer arrived at our factory gate and announced that he was forming a new TA Regiment of Artillery. He must have toured the town for hundreds of young men from shops, offices and factories to answer his call.

From our factory there was Jim Sneddon, Frankie Hardie, Forty Proctor, Albert Mead, Tommy Farrar and myself; from the offices of Armstrong Addisons came Norman Grierson, Bert Beatie and Tommy Denton; from Thomas Reeds the Printers came Tommy Brown, Bobby Guy and Wilf White; from Wilson's Glass came Charley Carney, Dave Wandless, Ernie Thompson, Fred Brass, Arthur Thompson, Harry Chatt, Robert Wilson and Peter Harvard. So, it was from all over Sunderland.

Hundreds of young men from all walks of life answered the call and I discovered that I was in the company of Eddy Crawford, John Scott, Eric Telford, Sid Maddison and Jack Madgwick who were classmates of mine at West Park School. Also, Fred Bell, Harold Bell, Billy Young, Stan McCulley, Billy Hunter and Viv Edge who were fellow choristers at Bishopwearmouth Church. So, I was surrounded by friends when we took the Oath of Allegiance at the drill hall on The Green.

We were expected to do four drills per week and were asked to choose to train as Gunners, Surveyors, Drivers or Signallers. I chose the latter and had no difficulty in mastering Morse Code.

We drilled and trained on the playground of my old Primary School (Rectory Park) and at Livingstone Road Drill Hall, but looked forward to our fortnight camp at Whitby: this took place on 26 August. Unfortunately, we were recalled to Sunderland on 1 September because of the seriousness of the situation on the Continent.

It was so serious that we were called up into regular service; we were no longer civilians.

For the first few months, the Regiment was stationed at Seaburn. Regimental HQ occupied Dykelands Road Drill Hall and 294 Battery was in the Concert Hall. 295 Battery used the Bay Hotel and Seaburn Camp.

With very little equipment, we trained as well as we could.

I was promoted to Lance Bombardier and sent to Darlington on a signalling course.

In February 1940, I attended a second signalling course at the School of Signals in Catterick.

Lance Bombardier Mr Len Gibson, c1939.

CHAPTER 2

On the Move

The Regiment was renamed the '125 Field R A' and was divided into two Batteries (294 and 295). I was put into B Troop of 294 Battery. Sadly, after months of training for Field Regiment work, it was decided by higher authority that we should be transferred to a Norfolk Division and become an Anti-Tank Regiment. Signallers and Surveyors were now redundant. It was a sad day for the regiment.

In the new order of things, the Regiment was divided into four Batteries (A, B, C and D). I was now in J troop of C Battery.

On a beautiful summer day, we arrived in Norfolk. From Thetford we moved to Catton Park on the outskirts of Norwich. After months under canvas, our Battery moved to the Bishop's Palace in the City Centre. From there we made trips out to the Coast where we manned defensive positions at Sea Palling and Mundesley. Our greatest activity there was to apprehend a crew of Germans who baled out and rowed ashore in a dinghy.

Photo: Taken at Livingstone Road Drill Hall 1939 -
Sgt Major Jameson, Paddy Lang, Cranmer, Les Barker, Bill Lawson, Nick Hutchinson, Tommy Cleghorn, Eric Telford, Allan Pratt, Butler and Johnny Glancy.

Norwich was an interesting city, and we enjoyed our stay there. Once a week, if not on duty, we could dance at the Samson and Hercules which was just across from the Bishop's Palace. Ernie Maughan, Wilf White and I went out together. We seldom went into the local pubs and if we did, it was only for one drink – usually in the Orford Arms or the Prince of Wales. The latter was the haunt of the pilots from nearby Aerodromes.

Photo of 294 Battery taken on the waste ground behind the Concert Hall - Seaburn
Bill Wallace, John Sugden, Nick Hutchinson, Ted Kidd, Arthur Judson, George Bennett, Don Mackintosh,
Joe France, Stan Crosbie, J McCready, Gerry Brennan, Gordon Timney, Sgt Judson, Norman Jefferson,
Peter Williams, Benny Phillips, Vic Threws, John Glancy, Paddy Lang, Maurice Ridley, A Butler, Les Barker,
Dick Austin, Norman Hannon, Tony Burnham, Wilf White, Ernie Tutin, Len Gibson, T S M Hockley.

One night Ernie was on guard. Wilf and I were lost for something to do and eventually ventured out of the Palace and wandered out to take the air. Wilf suddenly brought my attention to a pub called Whites. As Wilf's surname was White, we just had to go in. We were inside before we thought of money. We were the only customers and the bemused barman watched with interest as we emptied our battledress pockets and put the findings on the bar counter. After paying for two halves, we were left with one shilling and four pence.

There was a dartboard and we'd been playing for about half-an-hour when the door opened and in came the most glamorous girls we'd ever seen. They ordered their drinks, settled on the high bar stools and lit up cigarettes which were held in long holders. They were very smart and may I say expensively dressed and sported quite a lot of jewellery.

Wilf, who had not been able to concentrate on his darts since their arrival, then shocked me. He marched straight across to them and asked if they would like to play. Wilf, an only child and mollycoddled from birth, was ever an innocent. He even asked them "chalk or cheese" to decide who played with whom.

The young ladies had evidently played before and soon were throwing some good darts. I was so embarrassed I could hardly hit the board. At one stage, after I had my turn, I went to the bar to have one sip at my drink. The barman who had been watching us with some interest said: "Wait till oy tell moy boss. Wait till oy tell moy boss."

This puzzled me somewhat and I could not resist asking him what he was going to tell his boss.

"Two blooming squaddies with only one shilling and four pence between them playing with the most expensive prostitutes in the ole of East Anglia."

In those days, I had hardly ever heard of such ladies, and even the word prostitute was one I'd never spoken aloud.

As soon as I could, I grabbed Wilf's arm and said quite loudly that we had better get back to Barracks as we were on duty. Wilf was puzzled and reluctant to move but I practically dragged him to the door. Once in the street with the indignant Wilf, I was able to put him in the picture.

What a good giggle we had, and of course we still had our one shilling and four pence.

The Furlough

In December 1940 whilst billeted at Norwich in the Bishop's Palace, I was given the glad news that I had been given leave of absence. It was for 14 days and what was more exciting was the fact that I would be home for Christmas – and New Year – and my 21st birthday. I was told to pick up the pass at the Battery Office which was about a quarter-of-a-mile away through the city.

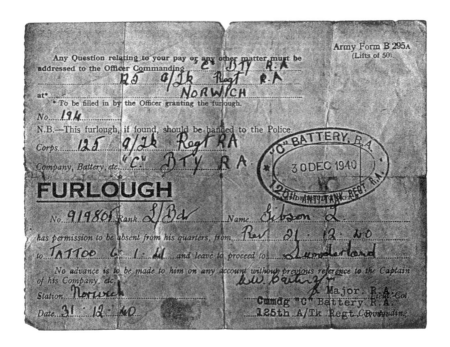

On opening the door, I was amazed to find a wall of fog. In fact, the whole of the city of Norwich was blanketed and instead of a ten minutes' saunter, I was faced with a daunting journey. The city traffic was almost at a standstill. Passenger buses could only proceed by following the beam of a torch which was held by the conductor who was feeling for the kerb.

After more than a year of blackout, I thought I was capable of finding my way in the dark, but this was worse. Eventually, I found the Battery Office, procured this precious furlough and set out to find my way back.

Sometime later, I was pleased to find myself in the entrance to the Samson and Hercules. I knew then that I must cross the same street. With difficulty, I managed this and started to feel for the Palace wall. I was pleased to find rough stone texture and follow it along until I reached the gate. How I went wrong from there I'll never know. I lost the path to the main porch and spent the next hour wandering the Palace grounds with its tombs, trees and gravestones. I stumbled over stones and fell into bushes. My face was scratched; my cap was pushed from my head; my battle dress was soaked. I finally touched wall and groped my way along it until I felt glass. It was a window and I wrapped loudly upon it. A voice from within called out, "Who's there?" It was Sergeant Ted Minto and I realised that I was outside the Sergeants' Mess. I now had my bearings, but best of all I had my precious pass.

Photo: Wilf White and Len Gibson.

Photo: Wilf, Ernie Maughan and Me
(The Three Musketeers).

Photo: Bill Wallace, Ernie Maughan, Len Gibson, Wilf White, Ted Willis, Bill Conlon, Gerry Brennan,
Bob Cranmer (8 of these men from our troop went abroad and 4 died in Japanese POW camps).

Photo: A break from training – Summer 1940 at Catton Park, Norwich
Jack Robinson, Norman Hannon, Wilf White, Ernie Maughan, Ken Wolfe, Len Gibson.

Photo: Relaxing in the sun –
Norman Jefferson, Tommy Old, Len Gibson, Tony Burnham, Ken Wolfe, Ernie Maughan, Doug Herbert.

I've lost count of the number of guard duties I had to do during my service days and usually they were boring and passed off without incident. One duty at the Bishop's Palace was the exception. As guard commander, I had to make sure that all men reported back to barracks by 23.59 hundred hours and to see to any who had had a little too much to drink. This particular night a small group arrived just before midnight but rather a little worse for wear. They went upstairs peacefully enough and I then expected a quiet night.

About thirty minutes later, a gunner came dashing into the guardroom shouting that someone had shot the cook. I sped up the stairs to find the inebriates staring in disbelief at the floor where the cook whose name was Proctor was lying with a pool of blood below his neck. A first aid dressing had been applied to the wound and I sent one man to phone for an ambulance and another to fetch the orderly sergeant.

After the ambulance had taken away the poor unfortunate cook, I arrested two men who owned up to being responsible and took them and the rifle they had used to the guardroom. There, Sergeant Minto and I had the difficult task of eliciting a true story of what had happened.

The room they were occupying was on the top floor and had a small window with a good view over the city. Evidently, there had been a challenge to hit the pointers of a distant church clock. One had loaded the rifle with a tracer bullet and, in carelessly handling the weapon, had touched the trigger. The bullet had gone into the shoulder of the recumbent Proctor and came out the back of his neck. Luckily, the wound was not fatal, but the regiment lost a cook!

A bandolier was hanging on the wall and somehow the bullet must have ricocheted around the room and damaged one of the pouches.

Some years after the war, I arranged a tennis match with the members of my staff. We chose Roker Park as the venue and when I went to book the court, who should take my money but an ex-member of the 125th Regiment, an ex-cook named Proctor! I surprised him by asking if his wound had healed, and he was interested to hear my story of how I arrested the men who shot him. Of course, much of it was news to him.

In January 1940 I was sent to Catterick on a course. Catterick was like Siberia. On the first morning I looked in the Lecture Room to see only Officers. I was about to go away when some Sergeants appeared. With one stripe on my arm, I felt insignificant.

A week after the course finished, I received a letter from the Chief Instructor. Across the top in large block letters it read: "WELL DONE YOUNGSTER. YOUNGEST IN AGE, LOWEST IN RANK BUT HIGHEST IN MARKS. I'd beaten the Officers and Sergeants!!

CHAPTER 3

On the Move Again

In extreme wintry conditions the regiment moved to Scotland. I was in the advance party. We lived in Nissen huts. Everything was frozen. When Major Cave-Bigley arrived, he moved us into a nearby empty castle: it was cold, damp and dreary but a slight improvement on the Nissen huts.

After serious manoeuvres, we moved to Selkirk, then Gourock where we boarded the liner *Strathaird*.

Out in the Atlantic, we were involved in a collision with the *Stirling Castle* and returned to port for repairs. In Glasgow we were billeted in Mount Florida Girls High School.

After a spell of fire watching in that great Scottish city, we moved to Heaton Moor, a suburb between Manchester and Stockport. From there we travelled to Liverpool where, for several weeks, we spent our nights in the dock area during very heavy air raids, and by day we were bussed to a council house estate at Huyton to rest. Sadly, during one blitz, three of the Regiment were killed, one of whom was Sergeant Viv Edge who had been a fellow chorister at Bishopwearmouth Church. The war had taken the first of my friends.

It was at Heaton Moor railway station that several men of our Battery noticed a huge poster. It was an urgent appeal for young men to be trained as pilots: '*The Air Force Needs You*'.

Without seeking permission from our officers, half-a-dozen of us wrote to the Air Ministry and within a few days received travel vouchers to go to Cardington. After a thorough medical and intense interview, I was given a piece of paper stating that I had passed fit to be trained as a pilot in two-seater night fighters. What really pleased me was the fact that I was fit. The Regiment moved before I could start that training and I was to learn after the War that my mother received a communication from the Air Ministry stating that I had failed to report for training and would be considered a deserter. She received this about the same time that the War Office said that I was missing believed to be a Prisoner of War.

I was promoted Bombardier and transferred from J troop to H troop.

From Heaton Moor, the Regiment went into North Wales to Trawsfynnd for target practice. Our aim with the two-pounder anti-tank guns was so accurate that we destroyed all the targets in record time.

Photo: C Battery at Tavernham Hall, Near Norwich
From left to right: Doug Herbert, Tony Burnham, Fred Laidlaw, Jim Wilson, Len Gibson, Wilf White.

Photo: J Troop at Heaton Manor
Back Row – Sgt Ted Minto, G Bennet, T Willis, Wilf White, Keith Suddards, Mike Conlin, Bob Stephenson, Fred Mills, Len Gibson, Bill Wallace, J. Roberts, Ernie Maughan.

Front Row – Jock Kirkham, Norman Hannon, Gerry Brennen, Bob Cranmer, Jackie West.

Huyton, near Liverpool
Resting between air raids
Sgt Davison, Keith Suddards, Bob Howie, Len Gibson, G Laing and Gordon Timney.

CHAPTER 4

Away at Last

Shortly afterwards we said goodbye to Cheshire and journeyed to Avonmouth from where, on 28 October, we sailed North up the Irish Sea on the *S S Oronsay*. After meeting up with several other vessels in the Clyde, we headed out into the cold and wet Atlantic.

I did a spell in charge of the machine gun posts and it was no easy task fighting my way forward in the teeth of the gale to visit the various guns. Taking hot cocoa to the gunners who were huddled in those boxes meant hanging the canister in the crook of my arm and pulling myself along the rails with two free hands.

Halfway across the Atlantic there was great excitement. Our navy escort left us and we were met by the U S Navy. There were destroyers, cruisers, battleships and carriers, and they put on a great show as they cruised past our convoy on either side, then did an about turn to come up alongside.

On 8 November we reached Canada. It was a beautiful sunny morning as we sailed up to Halifax. On either side of the estuary the brightly painted cabins among the pine trees presented a pretty picture. A greater spectacle was in store for us. In the harbour we transferred from our dull British liner to a US Ship named the *Joseph T Dickman*, and at night came the delight. We came up on deck to find the town, the harbour and all the ships ablaze with lights; no blackouts – such an illumination; we had not seen a city lit up for such a long time.

The lads wanted a singsong on deck so I took up my banjo. I was wrapped up in what I was playing and it was some time before I looked up to find that all of my pals had gone and I was surrounded by the crew's black sailors who were listening intently.

We sailed south. The weather became warmer and the lads became browner. We gloried in the sunshine. We called at Port of Spain in Trinidad but only the US crews were allowed ashore.

As we approached the Equator, the crew rigged up a huge pool and we guessed that someone was in for a real ducking. We were pollywogs (an Americanism for a person who has not crossed the Equator) and had to be initiated into the Ancient Order of Shellbacks. King Neptune and his entourage came aboard and for two days there was a constant procession of pollywogs paying homage to King Neptune and being lathered and shaved by Davy Jones and his helpers.

The American crew were great. They organised wrestling and boxing matches and showed British films. We got used to the orders that came over the tannoy: *"Now hear this - Darken ship - Secure from close quarters,"* and every night we gathered on deck to watch the sunset and hear the officer of the watch order the disposal of the day's rubbish.

We continued to sail south and after a few more fine days, we were hit by a terrific storm. The *'Joseph T Dickman'* was tossed around like a cork. We could hear the cargo rolling around beneath us.

On 7 December came dreadful news. The Japanese had attacked Pearl Harbour; our American hosts were devastated.

We were delighted to see Cape Town with its famous Table Mountain and even more pleased when we learned that we were allowed ashore. We'd been at sea for six weeks so four days on dry land was a welcome break.

The American battle fleet was now required for more important work and when we set sail we had only one cruiser to escort us: it was the *R N Dorchester*. In the middle of the Indian Ocean, the Americans gave us a marvellous Christmas dinner and a few days later we landed in Bombay.

I was absolutely fascinated with what I saw in Bombay. I was also appalled at the poverty: beggars constantly trailing after all the soldiers whining: "Backshees Sahib"; hundreds lying destitute on the pavements and in doorways; frail women carrying babies, tapping their naked bellies and crying for help.

CHAPTER 5

Wartime Memories
23 January 1942 to 14 October 1942
Singapore

On 23 January 1942, we were lined up on the docks in Bombay. The ship in front of us was nothing like the U S ship which had brought us there four weeks previously: this was the *Empress of Asia*, a very old boat which was so dirty that our Colonel refused to let us board. The Colonel was overruled by a higher authority.

I had a job to get up the gangway. On my back was a large pack with rolled ground sheet; on my front was my gas mask and cape; at my sides I had a small pack – water bottle and bayonet; over one shoulder I had a rifle and on the other my bulky banjo case. I also struggled with heavy kit bags, one in each hand.

It was very dreary below decks so Doug Herbert and I resolved to sleep out on deck just as we had done on the U S ship, the *Dickman*. We sailed south so knew that we were not bound for the Middle East.

On the morning of 4 February, we were awakened by a voice and were surprised to see just below us a naval vessel. On the bridge was an officer calling through a loud hailer, *"Get a move on Asia or we'll have to leave you!"* were the words we heard. With that, the vessel sped off.

After breakfast I went up on deck again to my favourite spot: right in the bow of the ship. The naval craft was not to be seen. It was a beautiful day; the sky was perfectly blue and the sea was so clear that I could see the bed of the ocean below me. We were in the Sundae Straits and on either side, almost a stone's throw away, were beautiful beaches fringed with palms which seemed to dip their heads as if saluting our passing.

What an exquisite place! What a wonderful world! Isn't it great to be alive! What a lucky person was I to be sharing this.

Suddenly, I was brought back to reality. The noise of planes caused me to lift my eyes to the skies: there were 27 of them and Japanese no doubt.

Hardly had the alarm bells sounded when several bombs exploded around the ship. From my position in the bow, I watched as great spouts of water shot up either side. They were close enough to cause the vessel to bounce up and down. The damage was not too serious. Some lifeboats were holed and plates were buckled.

As soon as the first bomb dropped, the stokers deserted their posts and the ship began to slow down at a time when we needed even greater speed. Half the lads in our Regiment volunteered to stoke the fires so that we could run the gauntlet.

The *Empress of Asia* had been built in Govan in 1912. She had made 300 Pacific crossings and had carried troops in the First World War. Little or no modernisation had been made and hence, was too old and too slow.

About mid-morning, we were struggling to keep in sight of the rest of the convoy. It was then the Jap planes reappeared. Once again our ship was the main target. Our gunners put up a huge barrage and it was an hour before a Jap plane scored any direct hits. Three bombs hit the ship, one passing through the lounge and dining room. Soon volumes of smoke poured from amidships. Lieutenant Bob Wilson was killed and two other officers injured. The others had to fight their way back through the smoke and flames to reach the open deck.

Our machine gunners did valiant work emptying magazine after magazine at the attacking planes and stayed at their posts until almost surrounded by flames. Some had to dive into the sea, whilst others slid down ropes onto the well deck.

Down below in the hospital, the medical officers and their orderlies had to resort to pushing patients through the portholes before escaping that way themselves. When the attack started, I was ordered below deck and joined the rest of my troop. We were a long way down and it was not very pleasant. We knew that the ship had been hit. We knew the ship was ablaze and we could not understand why we should have to remain so far down in the holds. We felt trapped. We felt inadequate.

We smelled the smoke and watched the staircase, anxiously awaiting an order to move up. It seemed an eternity before an officer appeared. We were lined up and started to make our way up the staircase. I had not realised there were so many steps and each one we trod was treated as a piece of territory gained. It was so painfully slow, but eventually we emerged coughing into the bright sunlight – into the noise, the smoke, the battle. Yes, a battle was still in progress. The Jap planes had turned their attention to the other ships in the convoy and repeatedly attacked our escort ship the *Exeter*. A few hundred of us were now crowded in the bows of the ship so as to escape the flames and heat. We cheered when a plane crashed into the sea. We applauded when the *Exeter* skilfully manoeuvred to cause Jap bombs to fall harmlessly into the sea. Our own ammunition was now exploding and adding to the noise of the battle. Some of our men were hit and received immediate first aid. A bombardier next to me fell wounded. A wood door was brought together with some rope. He was laid on the door and carefully lowered into the sea.

The ship was in danger of drifting into a minefield, so the captain ordered the anchor to be lowered. Some seamen released the appropriate mechanism but nothing happened: it was stuck. A line of us had to stand each side of the chain and hold a link each. Then, on command we jerked it up and down until it went rattling and screeching into the sea.

Meanwhile, the battle continued. Planes were trying to sink the *Exeter*. The *Exeter* at full speed, dodging falling bombs, was a sight to behold. Streams of tracer bullets sped into the sky from every ship around. For a while the *Felix Rouselle* seemed to be on fire. The flames on our ship were creeping nearer, the smoke getting thicker, the heat becoming unbearable.

The Colonel stood on a bollard and we crowded around him. He told us that we had to abandon ship. He pointed to a pall of smoke on the horizon and said that the captain reckoned that that was Singapore and was about eight miles away. He asked us to leave the ship and swim towards the smoke. SWIM? SWIM? EIGHT MILES?

I had never been in the deep end of Sunderland swimming baths. Oh, I had tried and tried many times, but never even managed to float. With a sinking feeling in my stomach, I went towards the rails. I removed by boots and helmet. Was it training or force of habit, but I placed them in line with the others. There was a line of boots with a line of helmets behind, all parallel with the side of the ship.

I ventured to look over the side: it was so far down. Some men were already in the water and swimming. There was a short rope that would get me part of the way down. The rope was rough and soon I learned that it was not policy to slide in case of burns. I reached the end and looked down: there was still a long way to go.

It took a while for me to pluck up courage and drop, but I hit the water and gasped for breath. Then I had a pleasant surprise, the water was warm. The piece of cork around my chest kept me afloat and I worked my arms the way I'd done on land drill. There were still men around but they were swimming confidently past.

The pall of the smoke seemed much further away now that I was in the sea. I began to consider my chances. How long would it take me to travel one mile? Multiply that by eight and it would be morning before I reached Singapore. That meant that I would be in the sea all night. Would I still be able to see the black smoke in moonlight?

We'd all been so crowded on that boat, but here in this great ocean we were lost. I kicked off my shorts and underpants as they were a hindrance. After what seemed an age, I looked around and could not see anyone else. What a lonely place the sea can be!

The noise of the battle subsided and the peace was only broken by the distant occasional shouts as friends encouraged stragglers to keep going.

Each man was now fighting his own battle – the battle to survive.

All manner of thoughts were competing for a place in my mind. What of my family back home? What would my mother think if she could see me right now? Would I ever see my dad and sisters again? Was this the end of the war for me?

What of the banjo left on the *Asia*?

I'd put my wristwatches, fountain pens and signet ring in the old leather banjo case for safety. I'd certainly never see them again. Where were the other lads from my troop? Were there any sharks around? What was the possibility of finding some driftwood that I might cling to? How far had I gone? How many hours of daylight left? Would I ever see Singapore? How long before I became too tired?

I must pace myself. I turned onto my back again. The sun was still burning hot. The Asia was still ablaze. I must use my legs more. I must be a long way behind all the others. I must keep going.

I could not believe my eyes when, after the umpteenth turn from a rest on my back, I saw some kind of boat in the distance. Was it real? Would I be able to reach it? It was a long way off. My heart pounded. What if it should go before I got to it? I renewed efforts.

What an anxious time; I could not take my eyes of that boat. I dreaded the thought that it might move. After what seemed an eternity, I got within hailing distance and became aware of other men in the water also converging upon the boat. It was with great relief that I reached the hull, but it was too high in the water.

At long last two sailors appeared with a loop of strong rope. I sat in this and was lifted aboard. I was ushered below decks to where medical orderlies were treating wounds and burns. I had not realised that I had burns on my legs. After treatment, I went up on deck. We were set for Singapore. What of the *Empress of Asia*? - a once great queen of the sea was dying.

What a time it took for our rescue boat to reach Singapore. It made me realise that I would never have made it. So, I stepped off that boat wearing only a shirt with my pay book in the breast pocket.

On the quayside was a reception committee. Some kind Chinese ladies were offering hot drinks and this was rather embarrassing. The hot sun had dried our shirts and the breeze was rather playful. We wanted the drink, but wished to retain our dignity. We were soon whisked away to quarters in some empty houses and issued with basic necessities: one shirt, one shorts, one socks, one towel, one toothbrush, etc.

We had been well and truly bombed at sea and now we were being bombed on land. Jap planes seemed to be always in the skies above us. The majority of the regiment were given rifles and bayonets and sent off into the front line. Our troop, 'H' troop were given the only four anti-tank guns available. To pull our gun, we had an old commercial truck. It had Chinese writing on the sides and onto it we loaded three hundred rounds of ammunition. We went into action at a place called Serangoon.

All day long shells whistled overhead. It was uncanny hearing their oscillating whistle just above our heads and imagining that we could almost reach up and touch them. Jack Robinson was sergeant in charge of the gun and I was second in command. The two of us slept very little at night preferring to be on alert.

During the first night, we heard voices and I crept along a gully to investigate, but they moved off before I could get near. Next day, it was rifles at the ready when more voices were heard in the bush and then a family of Chinese civilians appeared. We'd only been on the island a couple of days and were unsure about the nationalities of the population.

Could they be more Japanese? We had to let them pass. The next night there were more voices to be heard. They were definitely not English. Each time we tried to get near, they moved away. We held that position for two days and then an order came to move at speed; the Japs were encircling us. Back on the Chinese truck went the ammunition. There was only room for the sergeant in the cab with the driver, so we had to sit most uncomfortably on the three hundred shells. The truck lurched along the track and the shells rattled about.

The Japs spotted us and shells started exploding all around us. We reached a road which was full of fleeing civilians. Our driver had to forge a pathway through the middle. The gun, which was tied onto the truck with rope, swayed from side to side. Shells exploded on either side and our driver panicked. His foot was firmly pressed down on the accelerator, the shells rattled around and the gun swayed even more perilously as we went through the shell barrage at breakneck speed.

We reached our new position on Bukit Timah Road which was the main route leading to the city from the causeway. We hastily put the gun into action and unloaded the three hundred shells. Hardly had we finished when a shell hit a tree, the top of which fell onto the truck. The Japs had put up an observation balloon.

Number two gun, under Sergeant Kirtley, was behind us across the road. A shell hit a tree above their position and completely covered them. Number three gun was also under observation and they tried to hide in a small garden plot among huge potted plants. From our position we watched with alarm as the pots were systematically destroyed one by one by accurate mortar fire. When the barrage ended, we were amazed to see Sergeant Geordie Guy jumping up and down and waving to us; they were safe.

The next day we came under small arms fire. Gunner Thornton took it upon himself to investigate and had his bush hat shot from his head. Meanwhile, G Troop Officer, Lieutenant Mackintosh was killed by sniper fire and Sergeant Judson was shot in the wrist.

We had our eyes peeled on the road from the causeway expecting any moving object to be a tank. At one stage a truck careered towards us but luckily we held fire for it was a civilian truck driven by one of our men. Just beyond us it swung off the road and hurtled into the monsoon ditch. The driver had been shot and was bleeding: he died before he could be lifted from the cab.

Shells continued to fall and along the road planes made low flying trips. There was no rest for me at nights when I was not on watch. The continuous booming of the great guns and the sporadic noise of the firecrackers kept me awake.

On the morning of 15 February, all became quiet. After the noise of the past days, it was uncanny. Some staff cars carrying white flags went up the road and an order came for us to cease fire. I could not understand why and walked up the middle of the road to see if I might find an answer.

I would have risked being shot if I'd done this the day before. I met a brigadier and had the temerity to ask him what was happening, "Frankly soldier, I don't know," was his reply.

Word came that we were capitulating. It was to be an unconditional surrender. We could not believe it. We would all become prisoners of war. On our left flank was a troop of Singapore Volunteers led by a young Lieutenant who was a bank clerk in Singapore city. He was determined to fight on and asked me if I would join him. Before I could make up my mind, there was a rumbling and down the road came a long line of tanks and armoured cars.

We had been told that the Japs had no tanks and that most of them travelled on bicycles. We'd also been informed that they were tiny little fellows who all wore glasses. We were surprised to see so many six footers and hardly a pair of glasses among them!

We had no instruction about our gun. It was too late to blow it up. I took out the firing pin and carried it about until I had the opportunity to fling it across the road and into the canal. Streams of Japanese troops walked down the road towards the city centre. We could only stand and stare. Is it possible that we have surrendered to these? Has someone made a big mistake?

I spent a very uneasy night, and next day the order came that we must all walk to Changi. It was a long trek in the heat of the day. We had no food and no water. On the way we beheld some of the effects of the battle: bodies of our men killed in action, some halfway through a fence with rifles still in their hands; cattle killed and swollen to an enormous size; groups of civilians looking forlorn; half wrecked buildings.

When we finally arrived in Changi, we were put in Roberts Barracks and as there was no room inside, we slept on the concrete floor of the balcony. I slept soundly for the first time for about three weeks and the next day we were moved into the open. The barracks were required for the wounded that were being brought from Singapore. So, for a few nights we slept under the coconut palms.

The regiment was to get together for the very last time, but for a sad occasion. We paraded to bury Gunner McDougal who had died of his wounds. There were many wounded at Changi and I hated being on the hospital laundry fatigue. We had to collect all the dirty linen, often stained with blood, pile it onto a railway wagon and push it along the rails to the sea. There we washed these things as best we could in seawater. There was no soap.

Meanwhile, we were getting a taste of things to come - taste being the operative word, for we were given very little to eat apart from rice and this was most unpalatable. The sacks of rice had been stored with lime and when cooked, it turned yellow in colour. Even the smell was most unpleasant. This diet had an effect on our systems: we made water quite frequently, but went days without needing to go to the toilet.

3 April was Good Friday and on that day we were marched to Singapore to a place called River Valley: this was a camp in Singapore. The hut was infested with bugs and nearby was a stinking, stagnant canal. When it rained the bullfrogs made so much noise that we could not sleep. There was a row of standpipes under which we could shower. These were situated at the edge of the camp facing a row of Chinese houses and, as there were no partitions, it wasn't very private.

We were divided into working groups of thirty with three Japs in charge of each group. Musame was the boss. He was a dapper little chap and quite efficient. The next was Sito who was overweight and lumbered rather than walked. The third was a quiet insignificant little chap who would not say 'boo to a goose'.

Every morning was Tenko and we had to number off in Nipponese. So, we had to learn:

Ichi	Ni	San	Shi	Go	Rokko	Siji	Achi	Ku	Ju	Ju ichi	Ju ni	Ju san
1	2	3	4	5	6	7	8	9	10	11	12	13

The order for number was BANGO
The order for attention was TUESKI
The order for stand easy was YASUME

Some of our men were slow to pick up the Nipponese and were given a clout when they forgot their particular number. If a man was sick, we learned to say BIYOKI, and if a man had gone to the toilet, we said BENJO.

If he was suffering from dysentery, the words were TAXAN BENJO. Taxan evidently meant much or many, and the word for food was MESHI.

For the first few weeks, we collected handcarts; three to each cart and worked clearing away the debris of the city. This work gave us an opportunity to see life in Singapore: the people – Chinese, Sikhs, Malays, the Malay women following behind their husbands; the rickshaw wallahs in their blue pyjamas; the Chinese women balancing long poles on their shoulders carrying not only food but the wherewithal to cook it. I was fascinated by it all.

There were also sad sights and gruesome ones. On the railings outside some of the main buildings were the heads of Chinese who had offended the Japs. Those swords the Japs carried were not just for show.

Our captors presumed that they were humbling us in the eyes of the Asian population, but we disappointed them. We smiled at all the ladies, winked at all the kids and whistled while we worked. Whenever possible, we did a little trading when the guards weren't looking, and sometimes managed to purloin a few odd things which would be useful in camp. I think the largest thing we managed was a harmonium. It was great to hear Johnny Glancy play that instrument and it was to be extremely useful when we started to give concerts.

I was missing my banjo. It had been with me throughout the war: England, Scotland, Wales and a journey halfway round the world of India. I thought of it now, probably just a mass of rust and ash at the bottom of the sea.

I decided to make one and looked around for possible materials. Behind the Jap cookhouse was a crate with wire around it. I couldn't just pick it up in broad daylight, so I thought of a way to bring it to my hut. I collected all the pieces of string I could lay my hands on and tied them together. As we were passing after depositing our carts, I fastened one end of the string to the wire of the crate then when it was dusk, Wilf and I gently hauled on the string.

It took some time but we managed and I soon had the crate dismantled. I saved every part. I was in too big a hurry to make a proper curved body so ended up with a rectangle with the corners removed. I carved pegs like violin pegs and used a sharpened bully beef tin key to make holes in these for the strings to pass through. I flattened the wire to make frets and set them into the arm.

Charley Perry who was a French Polisher in 'Civvy Street' insisted that he polish it, and soon I was happy playing all my favourite pieces. I had tuned the instrument as a G banjo, but everyone who saw it referred to it as a guitar. I still had wood and wire left and thought of making an improved model.

I'd always fancied playing a guitar. They were coming into vogue and banjos were on the way out. I decided to attempt a proper shape this time, making a curved body with a good hardwood arm. When pulling our carts, we had often passed a factory and from the noise of the circular saws, I knew it to be the place where it would be possible to procure a good piece of hardwood. On the front of the factory, the name read 'Fogden Brisbane'.

The opportunity came quite soon. Charley Carney and Red Conlin came to me one day and asked if I would like to get out of the camp. I jumped at the chance, but how? They produced a piece of paper which read: "These men are allowed to collect firewood for the Japanese cookhouse."

They told me to collect a handcart from the Japanese lines and quite innocently, I walked into their compound and took one of their barrows. We pushed the cart to the gate and showed the piece of paper to the Japanese sentry. By the look of the chap, he probably had difficulty reading Nipponese, much less English, and the silly fellow let us out.

We were free on the streets of Singapore. It was a great feeling. We made straight for Fogden Brisbane. There, we collected all the little pieces of wood from the crosscut saw and filled the cart leaving a space in the centre. We kept some larger flat pieces to one side. From the factory, we headed for the Chinese quarters where we bought anything which would be useful in camp.

We placed these in the centre of the wood and covered them with the flat pieces. Having got safely back with our contraband, we decided to make more trips. Whilst in the factory, I kept my eyes open for a length of mahogany suitable for a guitar arm. When such a piece caught my eye, I surreptitiously pushed it with my foot along the floor towards the cart. It went on with the scraps and was quickly covered.

It was good mahogany and took a very long time to shape. Meanwhile, I had cut pieces of ply from the original crate and bent them into a circle wrapped with string. After work and evening meal, there was an hour of dusk when there was little to do except take a stroll around the camp to 'see how the other half lived'. I had a constant procession of sightseers interested in finding out how work was progressing: "When will it be finished? When will we hear it play? Where will you get the strings?"

I just had to keep going. Our trips to the factory continued. I often wondered how official these were. Red and Charley often looked round corners to see if the coast was clear before I moved with the cart, and we often dodged into a side opening if there were Jap soldiers about.

On one occasion we pulled into the Chinese quarters and the other two left me with the cart. Soon I had a group of curious children around: they were a mixture of Chinese, Indian and Malay and just stood there grinning. One suddenly produced a banana from behind his back and pointed to a piece of wood. It was changey, changey time! I handed over the wood and took the banana. They all dashed off and I thought that was the end, but a few moments later, they were all back and each one with a piece of fruit eagerly pointing to a particular scrap of timber. Before long I nearly had as much fruit as wood. I was really proud of the result and thought the other two would be pleased. In fact, they were disgusted: "What have you done? We have just negotiated to sell the load to a Chinese fellow for twenty dollars!" We had to dash back to Fogden's for another load.

Most of the civilians, especially the Chinese, wore clip clops: these were flat pieces of wood with a single strap across the toes. We called them clip clops because of the noise they made. I selected two scraps of wood and used two strips from an old boot to make a pair. When proficient at walking in them, I found they were cool on the feet.

On one of our firewood trips, I pulled the cart wearing these. I must have been the first European to be seen in them because as I walked down the roads, all the kids were pointing at my feet then dragging their parents out to have a look. However, on one occasion, I found that there were disadvantages to wearing clip clops for a group of Jap guards turned a corner and I had to throw them off and run like mad in bare feet.

We had occasionally passed a coffee shop which seemed very popular with the Singaporeans. The smells were too much for three hungry POWs and one day we finally surrendered. We parked the loaded cart in the roadway and ventured into the dim interior of a long narrow room. Coming in from the bright sunlight it was some time before our eyes became accustomed to the surroundings. We were in a café crowded with men of various nationalities and they all seemed to be smoking which made it difficult to see across the room. The whole place went quiet and we felt all eyes were on us.

There were drinks of various unfamiliar liquids on the tables, but Charley took it upon himself to do the buying while we found a table. Some Chinese fellows vacated seats, nodded to us, and went to sit with friends. The noise returned to normal and Charley returned with three steaming cups of what we presumed was coffee.

Gradually we ceased to be the focus of attention and we settled down to savouring the first decent drink for many a day. Suddenly the room went quiet again and we soon realised why. All eyes were now upon the doorway where a Japanese officer was standing. He peered inside then turned and walked to inspect the cart. We hoped that he would go away, but he returned and with hand on hilt of sword, let out a yell.

He spotted us and as soon as he'd made a few steps into the room, the rest of the customers departed. One minute that room was full, the next there was just him and us. Everyone else just seemed to fade away. As he approached, we stood up and Charley said: "Where's the note?" He himself managed to produce a now crumpled paper.

It needed smoothing before it could be shown to the officer who had been pointing to the cart and pointing to us. "Nippon shweezlbar – shigoto – ichi ni sang men," Charley explained.

This was supposed to tell the officer that we three men were working for the Japanese cookhouse, but Charley was no linguist. The officer perused the note: "Englisha ka?" "Three men, ichi ni sang," we said in unison. "Englisha ka – one – two – three?"

We all nodded together, and he took his hat off and put it on the table. What followed was like a pantomime as we taught him how to count up to ten in English. When he was finally satisfied, he put on his hat, adjusted his sword and strode out of the room.

The poor Singaporeans behind the counter watched him go. They had been as silent as the grave, but now began to chatter loudly in their own lingo. We decided that it was time for us to make a move, and we headed straight for the camp. We unanimously agreed to never again go to that place.

The Coffee Pot

The firewood trips were only made in our own time. Every day work went on as usual. One morning Musame led us to a large house with spacious gardens. Half of the party were left there to work and the day passed without incident. We had the occasion to take a peep into an open door and it seemed that Jap officers were going to live there.

That night after evening meal we were surprised to see our three guards arrive, Musame looked serious and shouted us out for Tenko. Reluctantly, we lined up and were kept to attention while Musame went along saying to each of us in turn: "You coffee pot?" We were flabbergasted. We were kept to attention for a further hour whilst the rest of the camp looked on. Then Musame repeated his coffee pot routine before dismissing us.

Next day Musame was extremely unpleasant and at night we were again paraded and again questioned about the coffee pot. By now Musami was furious and shouted a torrent of Nipponese before letting us go. We held a meeting among ourselves and everyone of us swore we had never even seen a coffee pot.

Next morning we watched as all the other parties left, then Musame shouted: "No coffee pot – you work hard!"

We did not collect carts but were marched at nearly running pace to a hill at the top of which some building was going on. Everything needed at the top of this hill we were made to carry at double speed. There were huge triangular frames of rough timber which were for supporting roofs and these were extremely difficult to manage. We sweated the whole day with only a very short break for rice and the Japs yelled at us the whole time. We longed for cooling drinks. We longed for the day to end.

The next day was even worse. We were taken to the docks where there were thousands of petrol drums. Even to walk near these was like entering an oven and we had to move them. Our hands burned as we touched them, and it was with great reluctance that Japs allowed us to use some rags for protection. The sweat poured from us and the guards screamed at us. We yearned for cooling drinks. We prayed for the day to end.

That night we could hardly stand when called out for another Tenko. This time a group of guards went into the hut and searched through our belongings. They returned disgruntled and dismissed us.

We were just about to settle down when we heard shouting and there outside on the parade ground was Musame and Sito, and stood to attention was an officer. Musame was slapping the officer's face and shouting: "English officarr – no gentle man! English officarr – no gentle man!"

Evidently, the only other person near the house where we had worked was a captain, and Musame had made a spot search and found the article amongst the officer's belongings. We learned later that the pot was solid silver and quite valuable, but we were never to see the thing that caused us so much misery. Needless to say, Musame was rather kind to us for the next few days and we had extra yasume breaks.

Sad news reached us from Changi: Doug Herbert died. We could hardly believe it. He had been working with me on the carts not so long ago until he fell from the top deck which was only a few feet. I'd lost a great friend.

Whilst in Singapore, in the year 1942, there were still a few elderly Chinese ladies who had been the victims of the foot binding practice. It was pitiful to see them walking as though on stilts. We had another occasion to work in the large garden of another mansion commandeered by the Jap officers and I was put to work by a fairly thick hedge. I had been busy for some time when I became aware of a figure standing on the other side of the bushes.

For a while I just carried on but finally looked through to see a beautiful Chinese dress and two tiny feet. I thought at first it may be a child but when I parted the leaves, it was an elderly Chinese lady with a very gentle face. She put a finger to her lips and the other hand passed something to me: it was a tiny handkerchief with a fancy border and colourful flowers in delicate needlework. I nodded and thanked her. It was very kind of the lady and I wondered if the giving of the handkerchief had any significance in Chinese custom. Really, it was the last thing I needed at the time. I would have been more pleased with a crust of bread, but I often think of that lady and her graciousness.

Another day I was sent to work on the godowns (warehouses). We loaded great bales wrapped in wire on to three-ton trucks. The Japs never knew when to stop and the load got higher and higher until ropes were thrown up by the lads working down below. I had been on the top arranging the bales and whilst the lads were tying ropes to the chassis, the impatient Jap got into the truck and started to drive off. Immediately I was in trouble. I did not have time to get down and there was a wire stretched across from godown to godown and hung about a foot above the top of the load. I could only try to lift the wire so as to pass over me and put out my right arm. The wire must have been live and I was thrown from the top. Luckily, my shorts caught on some of the wires around the bales and broke my fall. I was dazed. I had a burn across my wrist and my shorts were completely ruined and were my one and only pair. The Jap took me to another warehouse where I managed to find a pair from a pile of discarded clothing.

Even after managing to augment our diet by stealing or trading with the locals, our food intake was inadequate. Men were beginning to suffer from vitamin deficiencies. One third of the camp suffered what was commonly called 'Changi Balls'. The scrotum became extremely sore, red and weepy. Nothing could be done for them as there were no medicines available. It was worse during the heat of the day and the sufferers resorted to making fans and cooling their parts as best they could.

Our main food was rice and even this was of an inferior quality. Once or twice when I was too sick to go out to work, I was put on rice fatigue. This involved opening sacks of rice and removing the foreign bodies. For every four sacks, we filled one with insect cocoons.

Rice three times a day was monotonous and the cooks tried to give us a change at breakfast. It was known as 'pap' and was made from ground rice. We had two millstones to produce this and it was a long and laborious job. Even if the taste was only slightly different, the look of it broke the monotony.

There was some private enterprise. A few who fancied themselves as cooks made little fires on spare ground and fried rice cakes which sold for five or ten cents. Michael and Charley tried their hands at this. Charley was the cook and Michael the salesman.

We were always on the lookout for food when out working, but no matter how hungry we were, it was dangerous to steal from the Japs. Punishment was severe. It was also foolhardy to lift one's fists or retaliate when being beaten by a guard.

'Punishment' by Jack Chalker: an example of Japanese treatment.

One lad was beaten then tied up so tightly that when I met him a year later, he still had the scars on his wrists, ankles and stomach.

They were no respecters of women either. About sixty yards down a track from the edge of the camp was a shack made of pieces of rusty corrugated iron. An elderly Chinese lady lived there on her own. She was always pleasant and bothered no one.

We heard screams one day and ran to the perimeter to see the poor old lady being savagely beaten by a Japanese solder.

Of course, they could be cruel to each other. A sergeant could make a

36

corporal stand to attention and give him a good hiding; the corporal could do the same to a soldier; the solider could chastise a rookie. The Japanese officer was treated by the other ranks as though he was a god. They bowed low to him and were very subservient. So, it was no wonder that we were made to bow and if we did not, we were in trouble.

After working all day for the Japs, men had a little time to relax and forget their tormentors. Some who liked gambling played 2UP. The Aussies usually conducted the games and by the light of fire, men stood round betting on how two coins would land after being thrown into the air.

Sometimes, quizzes were arranged: hut against hut, or unit against unit. I was in the 125 Regiment's team with Major McKenzie, Lieutenant Walsh, and three other rankers. We were a fairly successful team. We also had people who were willing to entertain. Stan Clish from our regiment was clever at impersonations: his speciality was Charles Laughton's roll as Captain Bligh in *Mutiny on the Bounty*. He also remembered radio plays and directed one called *The Snatch*. We sat in front of a board painted to look like a wireless set and his cast spoke through holes in the board.

Conlin, Carney, Glancy and I organised a concert which was a success and that prompted us to put on a show which I called *Happidrome*. It was based on the popular radio show in which Harry Koris and Enoch appeared. I wrote a parody on their song We Three.

"We three we're not apart, we're a perfect company, Joe Stalin Winston Churchill and me.

"We three we're doing well, in the air, on land and sea, Joe Stalin, Winston Churchill and me.

"We'll beat the Bosh army, drive Hitler balmy, a tragedy?

"And in the Pacific, there'll be losses terrific, of that mythical Jap navy, you'll see.

"We three we'll set you free, soon at home you all will be (with) Joe Stalin, Winston Churchill and me.

"Who's me – it's Franklin D!"

What wishful thinking in those lines. Little did we know that we had three more horrendous years to endure before being home, and many of those at that concert listening to those words would never survive.

One man, however, certainly did make it back home, for when we were free and had reached Liverpool and were awaiting transport to our hometown of Sunderland, we met him. Johnny Glancy and I were walking down a street just having a look at city life when we passed a pub. There was music; the tune was familiar, the words were familiar and we went to find a POW singing my version of We Three!

There were still a few books around and I managed to read The Citadel, Gone with the Wind and a book of short stories which included The Monkey's Paw. I don't think I read another book for the next three years.

My guitar was nearly finished. One of the crowd who had come round frequently seemed more interested than most. He was a regular in the East Surrey Regiment and had married a Chinese girl. Sometimes at dusk he would sit near the perimeter fence and his wife would walk along the track outside. If there were no Jap sentries about, they would have a conversation. Many times they would just look at each other. It was sad to see her walking away in tears.

This East Surrey lad told me that I would have to learn chords and he mentioned names such as major and minor.

We were now working on a hillside digging out a level piece to make a sort of road. There were hundreds of us chopping into the hillside with chunkels and throwing the soil behind us. I asked the chaps next to me if they knew how to tune a guitar and as they did not, I changed places and asked the next fellow if he did, then I changed places with him and asked the next. I had to keep my eyes open for the sentries and dig hard whilst talking. Before the war there were few guitarists in Britain. It was not until the era of skittle groups that the guitar became widely popular.

At last I found a man who knew and with joy I tuned up that night. Now for those chords. Back on the hillside my question this time was, "Do you know what a major chord is?" I worked my way down the line again and finally met a man from the 148 Field Artillery who played the piano and organ. His name was Les McCulloch and when he told me it was 'Doh Me Soh Doh', I could have kicked myself. I had been in the church choir since the age of seven and every practice we had performed exercises singing up and down the 'Doh Me Soh Doh' and then raised a semitone and repeated. I'd sung millions of major chords!

I persevered and found every way of fingering these chords and when proficient wanted to know about the minor chords. On the hillside, I worked my way down the line again looking for Les McCulloch. From him I learned that all I must do is learn to flatten the 'M'. I then practised all my chords.

In 1939 I was sent by my regiment to do a signal course and one of the many things I was taught was how to make an emergency join of Don 3 telephone wire. One scraped the outer covering to reveal a rubber covering, and if one scraped further, one exposed strands of steel and strands of copper wire. "Steel for strength and copper for conduction," I can still recall the instructor shout.

I managed to steal a length of Japanese telephone wire and discovered that theirs was of similar construction. The steel strands were suitable for the top strings of the guitar, and I wrapped the copper strands around the steel one to make bass strings.

I now had two instruments and asked Wilf if he would like the first one I'd made. I also offered to teach him and he readily agreed. On the first lesson, I showed him how to hold the instrument and where to put his fingers for the first chord, but after a few minutes he had to stop; the inside of his forearm was covered with bug bites. Whilst busy with my second instrument, the bugs had made a permanent home in the first. I took the guitar out to the fire and held it over the smoke. It was a pleasure to watch those detestable creatures drop into the flames.

Bugs were a problem. They lived in the boards on which we had to sleep and all ways of killing them were tried. I made a bed for myself with four legs and under each leg I placed a tin lid filled with creosote; this certainly stopped them reaching me. Of course, another way of disposing of them was to catch them alive, put them in boxes and drop them in the Japanese huts whenever we could.

When our group had come to River Valley, we had left some of the regiment with the Colonel. The regiment was to be split further when a group was sent off to Formosa.

The Colonel and his party at Changi were to be involved in the 'SELERANG INCIDENT'. Because we could not sign certificates promising not to escape, the Japanese Commandant, Colonel Fukue ordered all POWs into Selerang Barrack Square. Starvation rations and minimum drinking water, plus the threat of disease when 16,000 men were forced to live on an area meant for 850 men, forced our officers to concede.

Meanwhile, conditions in our camps were getting worse: men becoming thinner and food becoming scarcer. Even the civilians in Singapore were feeling the pinch. I watched Chinese ladies sweeping grains of rice from the streets and noticed a change of attitude in the people.

The Singapore Times had been renamed *The Syonan Times* and was full of Japanese propaganda.

How long would we be prisoners of war? Would we see freedom?

News came that we were to move. Our working battalion was to go north to a new hospital camp; there would be better food, better huts and better medical care. It sounded too good to be true and that's just how it turned out to be.

CHAPTER 6

Thailand

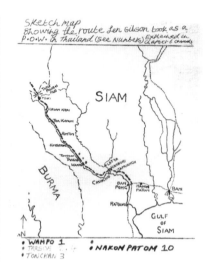

With all our worldly goods we walked to the railway station and there we stood in the burning sun awaiting our train. There was a long line of what looked like cattle trucks. They couldn't be for us? They were. We were put into these metal boxes, 30 to each; it was stifling inside. There was hardly room to stand, and the Japs wanted to close the doors. We would have all died. We complained and after a while the Japs gave in. We had no idea how long we would be on the journey, so we made contingency arrangements. We divided into three groups: A – would stand, B – would sit and C – would be allowed to lie down. We would change round every two hours.

When standing it was best near the door so as to catch the breeze. The metal sides were too hot to touch by day and too cold to touch by night. Some men were suffering from dysentery and it was a constant worry for them. At every stop or slowing down of the train, they were howled at and hounded down by the guards who thought they were escaping. "Taxan banjo" was the shout heard many times.

It was a relief to get out of that truck when we stopped for food. We were on that train for six days. It was a miracle that we were all still friends at the end. We stood on each other, tripped over each other other's kit. We could not see in the dark. It was truly a nightmare.

Whenever the train stopped or slowed down near to civilisation, men traded with locals for anything edible or drinkable. Many watches were sacrificed on that journey.

At last we reached our destination. It was a place called Bang Pong. We were marched into the camp and could not believe it. There were bare bamboo huts which were falling to pieces and the whole place was flooded. We were so thirsty and there were no taps; there was only a Shaduff and a Thai woman. I'll never forget her; she insisted that she draw the water herself and fill our mess tins.

Despite the deplorable conditions in those huts, we slept soundly for a few hours, the first for nearly a week.

Early on the morning of 24 October 1942, we had a breakfast of one cup of rice and one cup of tea, then set off to walk. We were on the plains of Thailand, and miles away in the distance we could see a range of mountains. The flat land was mostly paddy fields and the Japs led us across these.

We walked on the high strip of earth which separated the fields and indeed formed a wall to keep in the water. The strip of earth was only two or three feet wide and less in parts. All went well while the earth was dry, but we had a sudden downpour of torrential rain and the ground became soft and slippery. It was very amusing for the guards to see our lads slipping off the bund and landing up to their knees in the paddy. One went off every few minutes accompanied by a few shouts of: "There goes another! Any more for the skylark?" but the biggest shout of all was when one of the guards went in. The lads hooted with laughter when he tried to get out and fell back again. The guards were definitely not amused.

After a few hours we reached a road and had mid-day meal (rice, tea and gippo). Gippo was the name we gave to the stew which helped rice down. I once looked up the word and found the definition: boiled water to which ingredients are added. Some peculiar ingredients went into gippo. Of course, it was so little that it hardly flavoured the hot water and if you found a piece of meat, you thought it was your birthday.

That night we reached camp and had rice and gippo before going to sleep.

Next morning, it was more rice, tea and gippo and more walking. We reached Canburi by late afternoon. Next day, we ran out of road and hit the tree line. We'd walked across the plains and now were climbing the mountainous forest we had viewed some days ago. The leading Jap seemed to be following a telephone wire slung from tree to tree. At times we had to resort to single file and the pace set by the Japs carrying only rifles was too much.

Major Brodie was our commanding officer and he frequently complained to the Japs. The heat was unbearable and the going very tough. At least it was more interesting to me, seeing the occasional beautiful butterfly and listening to the strange noises of the jungle creatures. At night after rice, tea and gippo, we slept where we dropped and hoped it would not rain. Next day, we were off again, after our tea and rice of course.

At one stage we had to be ferried across a fast-flowing river in boats and we were so crowded we feared it might sink. Later, another river had to be crossed by a flimsy bamboo bridge. We ventured over singly at intervals and no more than eight were allowed on the structure at any one time. It swayed dangerously and there was quite a drop to the waters below. Many were scared. We stayed one night near a Temple and all night long were disturbed by tinkling bells and trumpets.

The further we went, the more tired we got and the heavier our loads became. The whole route became strewn with discarded articles. Many asked how I managed to carry my bulky guitar, but I would not part with that for anything. Men started to drop, and the doctors and medical orderlies worked overtime helping and supporting, and even carrying the serious cases.

On 28 October, we arrived at Tarso (The Soa); there were no huts for us to sleep in, but we'd got used to that on the way up. That first night we sat on some fallen logs until we dropped off them and slept. We spent the next couple of weeks cutting bamboo from the jungle and building huts.

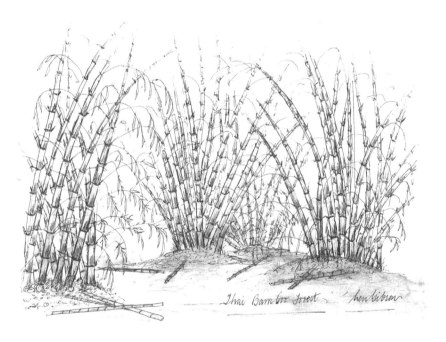

Thai Bamboo Forest   Ken Gibson

Michael Conlin, Charley Carney and I did get a task a little different, but we weren't happy about it. We were taken to one of the few huts which were already there when we arrived. It was superior to all the others. It was the Japanese Officer's. There was a pond in front of it and a tree to one side.

From the tools handed to us and from the mime performed by the guard who took us there, we presumed that we were to cut down the tree. He even waved an arm along the ground to show where the tree should fall. Not one of us had ever chopped down a tree before. We looked at the Officer's nice hut and we surveyed the pond. We studied the tree. That tree could fall anywhere!

The little saws were Japanese and sawed the opposite way to ours, but we worked away at the tree as best we could. We took turns with the saw, but it took ages. We were nearly half-way through when the guard returned and showed that he was disgusted with our progress. We attacked the other side of the trunk and got so far through that we were amazed that it did not fall. As we stood back puzzled, we heard it creak. It started to wobble, and we dashed round and tried to push it to the opposite side to the officer's hut.

But it came towards us. We dodged out of the way and sighed with relief when it missed the officer's abode by a few feet. Of course, we were a long way off the desired landing spot. We set about cutting off the side shoots and worked hard hoping we might shift it before the guard returned. When he did, he stood with his hands on his hips, shook his head and said: "No good ka."

On 17 November we embarked in barges and spent the whole night on the river. Why? I'll never know. We arrived at Wampo next day.

CHAPTER 7

Wampo

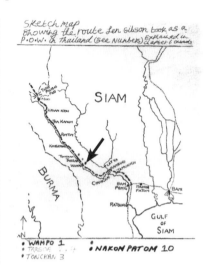

In our camp at Wampo, we were divided in B, D and F work battalions. D Battalion consisted of some regular soldiers and Malay Volunteers. The regulars were Gordon Highlanders and 9th Coast Artillery. The Malay Volunteers were civil servants, rubber planters, tin miners and bank workers who had formed the equivalent of our TA.

B Battalion was 18th Division infantry, mainly Sherwood Foresters. F Battalion (ours) was 148 Field Artillery and 125 Anti-tank. Our first task was to cut down bamboo, fell trees and clear away the brush ready for the rail track. Bamboo clumps were a nightmare. There were hundreds of sharp spikes on the branches and any scratches from these could result in sores or ulcers.

The stems grew so close together that at the base they pushed up the earth into a mound. To tackle a bamboo, one man was given a rope and saw and he had to crawl in below the branches trying to avoid the thorns. He had to saw through a stem, tie the rope around it then crawl back out.

A team of men would haul on the rope to extricate the stem from the clump. This process had to be repeated time and time again until all the stems were clear. There was still hard work to be done because the roots had to be hacked away and this was a formidable task.

When a wide pathway had been made, it was time to level off. Embankments had to be built and cuttings made through the high ground. We were set the task of doing one cubic metre per man. A rice sack on two bamboo poles (known to us as a 'tanker') was our main piece of equipment.

We dug earth out of the jungle, heaped it on the tanker and ran to tip it onto the embankment. When making cuttings the reverse happened and we disposed of rocks and earth onto the floor of the jungle.

The work was always under the eagle eye of the guards and if they were not satisfied with the progress, they would yell: "Speedo, Speedo!" and lash out with their sticks. Often the sick men who had been forced out to work would not be able to maintain pace which meant that those who were fit had to do extra; the cubic metre was a minimum - often it was nearer two. All this was achieved in unbearable heat and on empty stomachs. We did start the day with a pint of rice but within an hour, it had turned to water and our bellies were grumbling.

Frequently, the guards would find an excuse to attack a prisoner, and this was accomplished with much yelling and swearing. The unfortunate man just had to stand and take the punishment. To retaliate would mean torture and maybe death. Apart from beatings, men may be punished by being made to stand out in the blazing sun with a rock above his head.

Work and Play at Wampo

Some of the guards just looked for excuses to bully the prisoners. We used to say: "The peasant makes the worst tyrant." It was terrible to have to witness a comrade being beaten. Sometimes, a diversion was attempted. One particular ruse was for one man to jump onto the top of the embankment and shout: "Today is my daughter's wedding day." We would shout: "Hurrah!"

"Ten thousand pounds I'll give away!" We all responded with another: "Hurrah!" He would add: "On second thoughts, I think it best to keep it safe in the old oak chest!" This was greeted with boos and cries of: "You greedy!"

Of course, there was : "They're going to pull the pub down," and this could go on for much longer; this was sometimes enough to distract the Japs.

Every day started the same: one pint of Pap Rice (made from ground rice) and one pint of tea, followed by Tenko and a march off to work. The Foresters usually went before us and always whistled *Colonel Bogey*. Of course, the Japs would then call for all the sick men and harangue the doctors for not passing them fit to work. Malaria sufferers were forced out to work. One had to have an open wound or be bleeding to be excused.

At the end of the working day, the river called us. There we could cool down, wash away the day's dirt, clean our clothes and try to forget the railway and the Japs. There was a small beach 200 yards downstream from the camp. It was on the inside of a large bend in the river. We just jumped in as we were and stripped off when soaked.

After laundering whatever we'd been wearing, we threw them on the bank side and they were dry by the time we'd bathed. Mike Conlin had a novel way of doing his washing. As he removed a piece of clothing, he soaked it well and threw it at anyone nearby. Of course, they retaliated by doing the same and after ten minutes of this being thrown about Michael would put it out to dry.

It was here in this warm, yet cooling water that I finally learned to swim. After evening meal, there were a few hours to spend before lights out. Some men managed to acquire some fat or oil and with a piece of string to serve as a wick made a crude lamp using an empty can. By this poor light, men would play cards, often with homemade ones.

Others would light fires and sit out in the open. I often took out my guitar and played at the campfire and, if Charley Carney and Michael Conlin joined in, it would develop into a concert. These impromptu singalongs became popular and together with some of the Gordon Highlanders led by Snuffy Craig, we conceived the idea of giving a camp concert.

One of our friends in the 125 Regiment was Billy Arnold and he had an uncle in show business. He'd evidently seen many of his uncle's reviews and under his direction we put on a show called 'A Mug in London'. Charley Carney, of course, played the 'mug'.

The show was a success and we appealed for more artists. Frank Street - an excellent trumpeter, and Reg Dixon - an accordionist, were great additions to the party. I was approached by three Eurasian lads from the Singapore Volunteers who said they would sing if they could borrow my guitar. So it was that I became friends with Jimmy Scheerder, Sidney De Cruz and Salo ZuZarte.

They sang Hawaiian songs in harmony and became a very popular act. I listened carefully to their songs and watched Jimmy's guitar playing. To this day, I still sing their songs.

We used to practice in a little clearing away from the camp. There were artists and helpers. One helper was Tony (Oxbridge and Foreign Office) but content to just come along to keep the fire burning. Apart from myself, there were Michael Conlin, Charley Carney, Johnny Glancy, Billy Arnold and Jack Baldridge, who were Sunderland lads and Snuffy Craig's group of Gordon Highlanders, plus four from the Sherwood Foresters and the Singapore trio.

We thought we were doing well, but things changed when a certain Charles Woodhams came on the scene. He was a real professional and he took charge. He shocked us by announcing that there would be women in the next production. He argued that we were limited by having plays with only men, but with women, the sky would be the limit.

First, he wanted a leading lady. No-one said a word and we thought that was the end of that until Bill James volunteered. We rolled around laughing. Bill was an Australian tin miner. Not only was he built like an ox, but he had a huge moustache, and his voice – he could roar like a bull.

He actually was serious, shaved off his moustache and became a huge success in the part. Mind you, no-one dare laugh at him. Charles Woodhams was excellent with a needle and using the torn borders from worn out mosquito nets, he fashioned costumes.

Bill Latham, a London barber, teased out rope and made beautiful wigs. One practice night, Jack Baldridge and I were chatting to Pat Donovan when Charles Woodhams asked the three of us to stand together. We were of similar height and weight. "Now, I only want three more like you," he said. Next meeting he arrived with the three and said he was ready to start work. Only then did we realise that we were to be a chorus line!

Only then did we realise what hard work it was. We thought we were using all our muscles working for the Japs on the railway, but Charles Woodhams found muscles the Japs did not know about. Only Pat Donovan did not complain, but he was a professional boxer in Civvy Street. We practised to the accordion playing, 'I want to be happy'. I was definitely not happy about doing it!

However, the big night arrived. There were no front curtains. The lighting was supplied by two fires, one at either side of the raised mound of earth which served as a stage. The men sat patiently on the ground. When all was ready, Reg Dixon struck up the introduction on his squeezebox, and the six of us emerged in line and keeping perfect time.

This was a complete surprise for the whole camp and a roar went up which resounded throughout the jungle. The sick men in the hospital half-a-mile away wanted to know what had happened. So did the Japs and their officer Colonel Hatari.

The Scorpion.

Bamboo Spikes caused ulcers

Of course, they all wished to see the show and we had to arrange a repeat a few nights later. In fact, Colonel Hatari phoned his counterparts in other camps and they arrived by barge.

The Jap officers sat on the ground in front, the Jap other ranks behind them, then the sick men on makeshift stretchers, our officers behind them and then the rest of the lads. The show again was a complete success. At the end, the cast stood to take a bow and we did what we'd always done at the end of concerts - we started to sing the National Anthem. Immediately, Colonel Hatari stood up and shouted: "No King!"

We were dumbstruck and for a while stood like the proverbial 'tins of milk'. I had an idea: I whispered: "Let's sing there'll always be an England." This we did and the lads joined in. The Japs did not complain about this, but the Scots played hell!

One third of the party were *Gordons*. An extra meeting was arranged and it was agreed that we would sing 'Land of Hope and Glory'. This pleased everyone and even today, half a century later, Far East POWs stand when they sing this fine song at reunions.

What a fine diversion these concerts were: so contrasting to the daily grind on the railway track; for a few hours men could forget. Of course, it was back to work for us next morning. It was back to reality. Back to the heat and the toil and the Jap guards and the yelling and bullying.

Apart from dealing with the Japs, fighting off malaria and dysentery, surviving on the track and trying to keep fit, a big worry was food. Not only did we not get enough, but what we did get lacked variety.

In the morning was rice and tea; mid-day was rice and tea (usually brought out in containers onto the work site) and evening meal was rice and tea and gippo plus a 'doover'. This latter was the creation of Sergeant Towell, our chief cook. It resembled in shape and size a scone or rissole and was probably made from ground rice plus any pieces of meat and veg available.

Of course, there was so little meat that only flakes of it might be visible if one was lucky. After the rice was cooked and served, there would be a layer of burnt rice lining the kwall and this was removed with a wooden spade. Despite the fact that it was pretty tasteless, it was very much appreciated as it helped to 'fill the gap'.

There was very little edible in the surrounding forest, but we were always on the look out for anything to eat: it was known as 'scrounging'. Having Malay Volunteers in the camp was a bonus. Some of them had lived in this area of the world for a few years and knew a little of the flora and fauna.

One day as I was trudging back from work on the track, I observed one of them picking a piece of plant growing out of the dusty track. I asked him what it was and he said: "wild spinach". Whether it was or not, I do not know but from then on, I collected it. I used to take it down to the river and give it a good wash and carefully pick off the leaves. I say carefully because there were numerous sharp thorns. I would boil these in a tin of water.

It was extremely bitter and the liquid was simply awful, but I persevered and swallowed as much as I could. When I told Doctor Bennet about this, he applauded the idea.

One evening I was preparing some spinach at the river's edge when I became aware of spinach leaves floating past me. They were coming from upstream and there was a Chinese coolie with spinach, but he was retaining the stalks and throwing away the leaves. I moved up next to him, put my can next to his and after a little miming, we became partners.

All leaves went into my can and all stalks into his. After a lot of smiling and nodding, we parted good friends. From then on, I ate every part of the spinach except the thorns.

In the open spaces around our huts, there were small holes in the dusty ground and these were the exits and entrances for small lizards. Before emerging, they would pop up and spend some time before moving off; this was a danger time for them because our lads had laid traps. A length of string anchored beyond the hole and a slip loop round the hole, and a quick jerk and the poor lizard was one tasty bite for a POW.

Next morning, it was back to reality: back to the heat and the toil and the Jap guards and the yelling and bullying.

With Christmas approaching, the subject of food became more topical. We remembered Yuletide feasts at home and recalled our last festive feast on the US Joseph Dickman in the Indian Ocean. The Americans gave us a fine treat on that occasion.

But what of this year? Would it be the usual rice and gippo? Our hopes were raised a little when we heard that the camp was hoping to buy a beast. Of course, the only beasts we'd seen around this part of the world were those ponderous water buffalo, and the nearest were across the river.

A deal was struck with a Thai owner and when the time came, Charley, Michael and I were detailed to help a sergeant collect it. Why we were ever chosen, I will never know! We went downstream about 200 yards beyond our beach and half-way across the river met the Thai leading a most pathetic looking animal. It did not even look like the rest of the buffalos and was slightly pink in colour. We dragged and pushed it until we got to the cookhouse.

After a great deal of negotiating, we were given a day off for Christmas. I cannot describe how I felt that morning when we were awakened to Frank Street playing *Christians Awake Salute the Happy Morn*. There were tears in the eyes of many as they lay gazing at the atap roof above them and thinking of home.

We did look forward to that Christmas, but it was a catastrophe. There was the usual rice and floating about in the gippo were cubes of meat. These were the size of oxo cubes but were as tough as rubber. It was impossible to digest them. What a let down!

I decided it was time to spring my surprise on Michael and Charley. Before leaving Singapore, I had secreted a tin of meat and ten cigarettes in a pair of old boots. These boots were hidden under the bed slats and they could not believe their eyes when I produced the tin of meat.

Charley was the cook and he managed to scrounge some ground rice and made three pasties. They were the tastiest things we had to eat for many a day.

As they lay back feeling much happier, I gave them an even bigger surprise. No-one had seen an English cigarette since Singapore, and I produced a packet of them. They were delighted and did a little bit of showing off in front of the officers.

So ended our first Christmas day in captivity. We hoped we'd be home for the next. Little did we know - it may be just as well we did not.

Santa Lucia

Wampo 1942 and Christmas was near. Rumours were rife. The Japs were going to give us a day off to celebrate, and we were going to give a concert. My guitar was missing a fourth string, so I retrieved the length of hollow bamboo that I had hidden underneath the bed slats. Inside this was a couple of lengths of Japanese telephone wire.

I stripped off the outer covering to reveal the steel and copper strands and wound each strand into a coil. Having stretched one length of steel between two uprights of the hut, I set about the tedious task of wrapping the copper around it.

The afternoon sun was extremely bright and my shoulders and arms were burning. I was engrossed in the work and failed to notice a person approaching until a shadow fell over my hands. I looked up and there stood a Japanese sentry staring intently at the wire.

"Kurrah! Kurrah!" he shouted and followed that up with a string of Nipponese. He transferred his rifle to his left hand and started to aim blows at me with his right. At the same time he continued to yell. The noise, luckily for me as it turned out, attracted the attention of a Jap Corporal who arrived to investigate. He spoke a few words to the sentry who pointed to my partly finished string. This gave me the chance to pick up my guitar and I pointed to the vacant string on the instrument and then to the string I was making. The attitude of the Corporal changed. "Hanter Loueea! Hanter Loueea!" he shouted. "Hanter Loueea!" Was

50

this a Japanese swear word? I'd not heard it before. "Hanter Loueea!" he repeated pointing this time to the guitar.

And then it dawned on me that he was attempting to say Santa Lucia. I could not believe it. Here was a Jap who was acquainted with a Western song. I fingered the C major chord, and after one strum hit the top E and sang: "Come Now and Sail With Me. Over the Water. Santa Lucia, Santa Lucia."

The corporal beamed and nodded all the while I was singing. "Good Ka, Hanter Luceea," he said. After a word to his sentry, he went off – humming and seeming very pleased with himself.

How fortunate for me that I'd met probably the only Jap in Thailand who knew a western song.

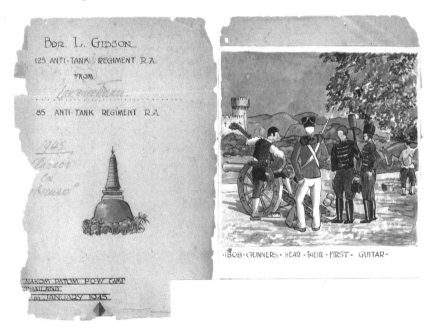

Birthday card made in camp and given to Len Gibson by Laurence Turner who later became M.P. for Oxford (he resigned over the Suez crisis in 1956).

With so many Scots in the camp and our own Sunderland Regiment, a lot was expected on New Year's Eve. Hogmanay was for celebrating with a few drinks, but that was out of the question at Wampo. Except for the Japs talking of Saki, no-one even mentioned the hard stuff. With Snuffy Craig and Tammy Cambleman, their friends were sat around a fire and talked and sang until midnight. Snuffy sang *Strange Names* and they all attempted to get through *Tam o Shanter*. We finished with *A Good New Year to One and All.*

Michael, Johnny, Charley and I made our way to our own hut. We were met by our Aussie Prima Donna, Bill James. He'd been looking for us. He asked if we had anything that would open a bottle. We could not believe it. He did have a bottle. In the bright moonlight, we saw that it was a dirty looking thing without a label.

When we asked him what it was, he just said: "Jungle Juice. We'll manage." Holding the bottle in his left hand, he proceeded to strike the bottom of the bottle with the heel of his right hand. After about an hour, we were prepared to leave him, but he insisted we stay.

On he went and then suddenly just picked out the cork out of the top of the bottle. We were all anxious to taste the contents, but after one tiny sip, I decided that it was not for me. Michael and Johnny were not very keen and Charley soon capitulated. We left Bill to it!

He must have finished it off himself. I don't know what was in that bottle, but it had an amazing effect on Bill James. For three days he was like a wild man. He armed himself with an axe and menaced anyone who went near him. The two Aussies who shared his hut went into hiding and even the Japs kept their distance. They thought he'd gone mad. I'm glad I just took one sip of that "juice".

A few days later, I went down with another dose of malaria. This was about the sixth time since arriving at Wampo, and one early morning after I'd sweated all night, I longed for a cool bathe. I wandered out of the hut in a daze. No-one else was astir. I could just see my way down the path to our usual bathing place, but when almost there, I noticed some dark shapes where we normally left our clothes to dry.

Who's been leaving logs on our beach, I was thinking to myself, when suddenly some of the shapes moved; they were alive, but what they were I'll never know for I did not stay long enough to find out. I was amazed to think that we were sharing our lido with the creatures of the jungle. We were on the day shift and they were on the night. I resolved never to go night bathing again!

As we had no water bottles, we used lengths of bamboo to carry water. Bamboo consists of a series of cavities separated by nodes. With a strong stick, one could smash through these to increase the capacity. So, how much water you required depended upon the number of nodes you knocked out.

We would fill these whenever we went down to the river to bathe. They could then be hung in the hut for when we needed to rinse our hands or do a little cooking.

CHAPTER 8

South Tonchan

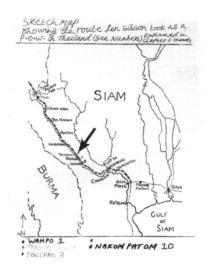

We were on the move again, to where? The Japs never divulged such information. "All men go!" they would say and wave an arm in the direction they wished us to move.

Part of the route was along the rail track and part along a jungle path. All we knew was that we were going "up country" to another camp. We soon began to feel the heat and wondered how long the journey would be. There were sick men struggling to keep pace. They wanted to stay with their mates no matter.

What a surprise we had when we finally arrived at our destination. There were TENTS. We had always had bamboo huts. A clearing about the size of a football pitch had a small river running down the middle, and on one side were rows of tents and across the far side in one corner, were bamboo huts.

After we'd been sorted out, 16 to each tent, we were set to work. The site had to be cleaned, wood collected for the fires and water brought from the river for the cookhouse. We were aware that Michael was missing from these fatigues, and it was close on mealtime before he returned.

"Dodging the column. Swinging the lead," jibes were aimed at Michael but Michael looked very serious: "You should see in those huts over there. That's where I've been. They're full of sick men and they're like skeletons. The Japs have just left them. They've had no music or entertainment since they've been here. I think we should do something for them."

Michael was so sincere that we took him seriously and planned our strategy for the night. After we'd eaten our rice and gippo (the usual evening meal), we trooped across the little bridge that spanned the river, dragging bundles of dead bamboo and carrying guitar and torches.

We chose a spot in the clearing about twenty yards from the sick men's huts, heaped up the dead kindling and set it alight. A Jap sentry appeared out of the jungle to see what was afoot and must have got quite a shock when we started to dance around the fire singing Come and Join Us.

Our Come and Join Us medley was made up of Salvation Army songs which we had learned from their bands when playing in our streets on Saturday nights, *Give me oil in my lamp*, *Please put a penny on the drum* and *Sunshine corner*. With the Jap sentry looking on in bewilderment, we pranced around until Charley was almost on the point of collapse.

At last what we had hoped for happened. Several skeletons emerged from the huts and walked unsteadily towards us shielding their eyes from the brightness of our fire. For a while they stood staring at the ground in front of them, then slowly sat down. Once their eyes became accustomed to the glare of the fire, they looked into the flames and not us. Red and Charley went straight into their routine doing all the jokes which usually brought roars of laughter. The audience was unmoved.

The rest of us took it in turn to stir some reaction, but without success. Even Charley's impersonation of Shirley Temple singing *Good Ship Lollipop* failed to move them – or so we thought. When we performed our final piece and thanked them for listening, they responded with an applause which, though not vigorous, was probably done with the maximum strength left in their frail bodies.

We had to help some of them to their feet and after just a nod of their head, they returned to their dreadful huts. So ended our first night in South Tonchan. Next morning, it was back on the railway. Our task this time was "hammer and tap". We had to work in pairs and each pair was given a long chisel and a heavy hammer.

Holes one metre deep had to be driven into the hard rock. We took turns sometimes holding the chisel and sometimes wielding the hammer. Periodically, the Japs would thrust a stick into the hole we'd filled and yelled and bullied if the depth wasn't enough.

When sufficient holes were ready, they put in charges of dynamite and we would run for our lives into the jungle to escape the shower of rocks. There were often injuries when the Jap engineers set off charges from behind their screens without allowing sufficient time for us to scramble to safety.

The work was very hard and it was also hot – extremely hot; it was like being in an oven. Of course, all the broken rocks had to be cleared from the track and deposited in the jungle. These were jagged as well as hot and for those of us with bare feet, the going was tortuous.

There were often beatings when the guards weren't satisfied with progress. John Glancy who sang with us on that first night suffered the wrath of one particular nasty guard. The latter used one of the heavy chisels and hit poor John on the head with it.

When work was done and we'd had our meal of rice and gippo, the sun was down and several campfires would be started. It was miserable inside the tents with no lighting, so around these fires we would sit and chat.

Sometimes, of course, we would have to be in those crowded tents and it was on such a night that I first met Harry Thorpe. We'd run out of conversation when a voice was heard: "Hot sweet coffee! Ten cents a cup!"

We just had to rush to open the tent flap and the voice was heard again, but more intimately: "Church service in ten minutes' time."

Padre Thorpe

Of course, there was no coffee and the voice was that of Padre Harry Thorpe. It must be Sunday. All the days were working days to us and we forgot Sabbaths. The Japs worked a ten-day week.

Some of us followed the Padre to a little clearing he used as a church, and braving the mosquitoes listened to the chap who had lured us there with dreams of hot sweet coffee.

He was a quiet spoken Australian and had a down-to-earth sermon to deliver. A group of us promised to meet him again next Sunday, but I was to meet him before then. He realised that I had the only musical instrument in the camp and came to me with some alarming ideas.

He not only wanted me to accompany hymns, but to play gentle music during communion services. He also listened in on camp singalongs and chose certain songs which described a picture or contained words which could be used to illustrate a sermon.

In spare time I helped him with his church. We made a rough altar and set up a bamboo cross above it. We also arranged fallen logs to act as pews. I doubted at the time if our efforts would be appreciated, or if those pews would ever be filled. Little did I know that this small clearing would become a vital part of the camp.

We returned from work one night to be assembled in that place by our own officers. We were numbed by what they had to tell us. A terrible disease had hit the camp – CHOLERA. We'd heard of the horrors of cholera epidemics and now we were at the mercy of one – with no medical supplies and no hospital equipment capable of fighting it.

We were advised to boil all water and not to bathe in the stream. All work on the railway ceased because the Japs were running scared and steering clear of us as much as possible. They retired to their own quarters and would not allow any POWs near them. They covered all pathways and entrances to their camp with lime.

Next night, there were only 14 in our tent.

Cholera

Two of our comrades had been isolated, and next day we learned that they had died. It was as swift as that. That same night there was another spare sleeping space in our tent. Three of us who were left were detailed for a special task. We had to collect a mass of dead bamboo or any wood which would burn.

The first of the cholera victims had to be cremated. We did not cherish the work, but collected a body wrapped in a sack and placed it on the pyre we had built. The work took all night. It seemed the body would never burn.

Our task the next day was much more pleasant. The doctors decided to give all cholera patients saline injections and they needed distilled water. A "man of the moment" came forward; one of the Malay Volunteers was a pathologist and our job was to assist him. Empty quinine bottles, bits of tube, hollow cane and our fire served to produce the saline which the doctors required. Of course, it took time but how thrilled we were when the first drops fell into the bottle; how impatiently we waited for that bottle to fill; how triumphantly we presented it to the MO.

The saline solution was dripped into the vein of a patient's foot; this evidently served to put liquid into the body which had become dehydrated by the disease. Meanwhile, men were falling ill and being taken to the isolation unit where they lived in agony for only two or three days. We were shocked when Johnny Glancy became ill and was taken away. The camp became as quiet as a graveyard. Sad faced, worried men avoided each other and wondered who would be next, or even if we all would die? At night we sat staring into campfires until sheer fatigue made us retire to our tents where first impulse was to note the vacant spaces and pray for those who were no longer with us.

After one week 98 of our group had died and of the 16 in our tent, only nine of us remained. We lay in the dark listening to the moaning of those awaiting removal to isolation and noting every movement within our stomachs.

John Sugden and I spent most of our civvy lives in church choirs and for several nights took to singing anthems we knew. At other times men would have been prepared to throw boots at us for even singing hymns, but on these occasions we were listened to.

At one time when all was silent throughout the camp, a voice was heard proclaiming: "Hot sweet coffee". Of course, it was Harry Thorpe. He chatted to us for a while and told us of a brave few who were working tirelessly in that dreadful ward and doing everything possible for those unfortunate sufferers. Tomorrow was Sunday and he asked us to join him in a special service to pray for the sick.

But we had a terrible night after the Padre had departed. We'd hardly closed our eyes when Charley dashed out of the tent and returned sometime later and lay moaning. After a while he went off again but this time he did not return. Red and I went to look for him. He was lying on the ground holding his stomach and groaning. He had not reached the latrines and wanted to go again, so Red and I helped him go to the bog and held onto him. Another figure came dashing towards us: it was Sergeant Bert B; he was in a similar plight to Charley. We guessed the worst, and Red went for the MO. His verdict confirmed our suspicions: it was cholera but he requested us not to tell Charley or Sergeant Bert.

We spent the rest of the night helping Charley to and from latrines and trying to convince him that he did not have cholera.

The next day the little clearing we'd made as a church was full. All those logs we'd arranged were occupied and crowds stood silently around. After a hymn and some prayers, Harry told the story of Columbus and of his voyage to the New World. He spoke of the fears of the crew and the threats to mutiny. "Give me three days," he pleaded.

Harry proceeded to match the situation with our own predicament. "Have faith in God. Give him three days." He certainly gave us hope and I noticed the change in the faces of those around me, and believe it or not, there was some good news! The Medics announced that there were no new cases. Those words, "No new cases" went round the camp like wildfire. Men began to speak to each other; there were smiles, even laughter. The whole camp came alive again.

Meanwhile Charley was seriously ill for a few more days and it was pitiful to see the man who was always trying to be cheerful and make people laugh in such a state. The epidemic, however, was abating and we cheered him with the news.

Those of us still fit were paraded and given picks and shovels. The task was a most unpleasant one: there were forty bodies to bury. It was impossible to burn them and they were to go into one large grave. We chopped away the brushwood and started to dig. To our dismay, we hit solid rock almost immediately. Our orders were to bury the bodies deep and we laboured all day in terrific heat, always conscious of the heap of rice sacks containing the victims of the dreadful cholera.

The sweat poured from us and this caused us to be very popular with certain insects that I'd never encountered in any other part of the Thai jungle. In fact, it caused some amusement when it first happened. When we stood up we all looked as if we were wearing ties on our otherwise bare torsos. Everyone of us had a cluster of harmless little bees which were busily and happily drinking from the perspiration running down the middle of our chests. We referred to them as "sweat bees".

We laboured hard even without any Jap sentries watching over us and finally reached a depth we thought adequate. Then began the odious task of placing the bodies in the hole. We had miscalculated. The grave was filled and there were bodies left, so we had to resort to covering up above ground. We were glad when just before dark the job was done.

Meanwhile, news came that Johnny Glancy was recovering, but we were not allowed to visit him. I had an idea: I would make him a cake. First, I would need an oven. The answer lay in a kerosene can. I dug a hole in the bankside large enough to light a fire and place a can above. Then I covered this with the earth I'd taken out. I bent the lid of a second can to form a shelf and managed to fashion a rough baking tin out of the rest.

With some ground rice, one precious hard-to-come-by egg, some water and a prayer, I lit the fire, put the cake on the shelf and closed the lid of the kerosene can. I made sure that the tin was well covered with clay and that my little hollow bamboo chimney was working. After a couple of hours, the cake looked rich and brown and Don Mackintosh agreed to get it to Johnny.

Later, when Johnny was released from quarantine, he showed me the scar where the saline solution had been injected and told me of nearly breaking his teeth on a cake which was so delicious on the eye, yet so hard on the molars.

The cholera passed but evidence of it remained. Days afterwards we would come across bodies of Indian labourers. Some were lying where they had died and some were sitting propped up against trees. There were no doctors with them and although they were the responsibility of the Japanese who had forced them to work, they had been left to face the disease without any help whatsoever. They had not known what was wrong with them and had just wandered off leaving them to die alone and in agony.

Cowboys

A few days later we could hardly believe our eyes. More than a dozen skinny cattle came wandering up the track and into the camp. I did not know it at the time, but my life at South Tonchan was to change because of them. The camp commandant was known to POWs as the "Tiger" and he wasn't given that title for nothing. He rarely showed his face and when he did, he was usually in a terrible mood so everyone kept well clear of him.

I was on my way to early morning Tenko when the Tiger and a guard came into view. "Soja," shouted the Tiger, and when I turned, he was pointing at me. The guard made the normal wave of the hand which meant "Approach" and I had to go to them and bow. "You soja, you cowboy. You find grass!"

I had been chosen to look after the cattle. I was astounded. I knew nothing about cows. Of course, the camp was unfenced and the beasts could escape so I had to work like mad making a makeshift corral. Meanwhile, I was offering them young bamboo leaves but they did not seem to like them.

The Tiger had said grass and it was imperative that some suitable fodder was found, as the beasts were so thin and starved. The Tiger came next day and gave a cursory glance at rough fence and another at the cattle. "No good ka!" He put his bunched fingers to his mouth to indicate food and walked off.

I knew that finding grass was nigh on possible, but I had to appease the Tiger. The jungle was dense and I knew it was easy to become lost, so I tried to walk in a straight line and leave as many clues as possible so as to find my way back.

The foliage at times was so thick that I could only see a couple of yards ahead. I often thought of turning back, but then thought of the Tiger. I pressed on, pushing foliage from my face and snapping the odd twig. Then suddenly I came to an abrupt halt; I was on the edge of a small clearing.

I stood stock still taking in my surroundings and became aware of a different mass of colour among the greenery, and there it was: the largest eye I'd ever seen – and it blinked. I did not move a muscle, then suddenly there was a crashing through the undergrowth on the other side of the clearing.

That was enough for me. I did an immediate about turn and ran back as fast as I could. I was relieved to find the corral, but the sight of those starving beasts reminded me that I had not completed my task. Would the Tiger bother to check? Is there any grass at all? After all, bamboo is grass and to exist in the jungle it needs to grow fifty or sixty feet.

I resorted to collecting the youngest leaves of the bamboo and hoped my charges would survive. Two days' later, a person arrived and announced that he had been detailed to help me. He turned out to be a sergeant and I could only suggest that we improve the corral: this we proceeded to do.

Now, one of the smallest cows in the herd was a dark brown colour and it had a tiny calf. This little creature must have been born on the way up to this camp; it was so small. From it I learned that their tongues were not like ours. I always made sure that it got first choice of the young bamboo leaves and it took to following me around, and soon I discovered why. Whenever I stood still or bent down to pick up leaves, it would run its tongue up the length of my legs. It was like being rubbed with rough sandpaper. It made me jump every time.

We were called to parade one morning for a medical and were surprised to see that Japs in white coats had tables, all prepared with an assortment of paraphernalia. We all had to suffer the indignity of bending over whilst Jap medics went along the lines pushing glass slides into us. Meantime, our herd started to decrease.

Paddy Eagan, accompanied by a guard, came along and studied the beasts. After more than a little trouble, he managed to rope one and take it off to the Jap cookhouse.

All the meat was used by the Japs, but any they did not want was put in our gippo. We were lucky to taste a difference in the flavour and extremely fortunate if we found a grain of meat. I lost my helper; the results of the recent tests proved that he was a cholera carrier and off he went and I never saw him again.

Every few days the Jap and Paddy would come for a beast, but I always prevented them from taking the mother of the calf. Sadly, of course, there came a time when only mother and calf remained. I was reluctant to let them be killed and on the morning that Paddy was due, I let them out of corral.

An order came that I personally had to deliver the beast to the Jap cookhouse: easier said than done. That cow must have known what was to happen! It would not let me near it, and it took me all morning before I managed to corner it and put a rope on it. I dragged the poor beast out of the jungle and by the time I reached the clearing of the camp, the lads were sitting around having their meal.

The beast then went off at a gallop dragging me at speed and doing something which I least expected. Whenever I was level with its hindquarters, it back kicked and it caught me like this several times. My legs were black and blue for days afterwards.

I was hanging on for dear life and everyone in the camp was enjoying the spectacle. The creature even dragged me across the stream and then back again. I finally managed to stop the creature when it returned to the jungle. I tied the rope around a small tree and held on until help arrived. So ended the job I had quite enjoyed, but next day it was back to work on the track. Really, I admitted to myself, I was not cut out to be a cowboy.

The Compressor

I walked out to Tenko next morning with Jack Baldridge. Jack and I had been lifelong friends. We'd attended the same Primary School, passed our eleven-plus, attended the same secondary school, and always accompanied each other on TA drills.

He was good natured, a happy go lucky type and a pleasant workmate. We stood on the end of the line and when Tenko was finished, a Jap signalled us to pick up two saws and an axe and follow him. After a ten-minute walk along the track, he stopped at a piece of machinery: it was a compressor. We wondered how it came to be there, but soon learned where it was going. It was needed on the rail track and our task was to cut a path for it through the jungle.

The Jap plotted the route and we set to work felling small trees and cutting away offending branches. For about an hour the Jap helped us with the work and seemed pleased with the progress. We tested our path by dragging the compressor up to that point.

"OK ka-more," said our guard and he pointed the way ahead. He then went off in the direction of the camp. Jack and I were happier working without him but often strayed from his straight line when a large tree blocked the way. By late afternoon we could hear the noise of the work on the railway, and all was going well until we came across a rotting log which was barring our path. We had to lift it clear.

"Nicky, nicky, nack – which end will you tack," joked Jack using a jingle we'd used in the infant school yard. "I'll have this end because it's bigger," quipped Jack and he gripped the log with both hands not noticing a scorpion. Having experienced a scorpion sting, I knew what pain Jack was about to endure. For the remainder of the day, he was in agony, but the work had to be completed so we soldiered on.

When at last we pushed that compressor onto the side of the track, we made our way back to camp; back to a good night's rest for me – but a painful one for poor Jack!

On the Move Again

On 28 July 1943, we were under orders to move again. On that day, I was having my umpteenth attack of malaria and Jack was really ill with dysentery. We were not sad to be leaving; South Tonchan had not been a happy camp. We had lost many of our comrades in the cholera epidemic. In spite of this, we were still anxious about the future. Our next camp might even be worse.

Emotive: Two working men, Konyu River Camp. By Jack Chalker.

We assembled on the road and were disappointed to note that the Japs faced us up country and not down as we had hoped. Jack was too ill to face a long trek but insisted that he came with us. We helped him to his feet so that he could join us and the column moved off. Hardly had we gone fifty yards when he had to hobble off into the foliage.

I waited behind only to be harangued by the guard. I pointed into the jungle, "Ichi man bioki, taxan banjo," I shouted. The column was halted temporarily until Jack emerged. Another hundred yards and Jack was off again; this time the guards were furious. When it happened again, the guards were ready to be violent.

After a short discussion among themselves, they resolved to leave us behind. Jack and I watched them out of sight and hoped we'd manage to find our way. I still had my guitar slung over my shoulder and when Jack was on one of his visits, I started to play.

"Do you know Jack of Diamonds?" said Jack as he came out from the bush. When I replied that I did not, Jack said he would teach it to me. So, we spent the next few hours wandering along the track, Jack only managing a few bars before wandering into the bushes and I trying to find the chords for his song.

We must have presented a most unusual picture.

When the sun went down, the jungle became ominous and we tried to make more speed. The track became more difficult to follow so it was with immense relief that we heard voices and sighted the flickering lights of Tonchan. We were too late to find out which hut we were assigned to and so lay down by the nearest fire and stayed there until dawn.

Tonchan

Next day I could not stop shivering. The following day I sweated. At night I was delirious. Jack's silly song troubled me: "Jack o diamonds, Jack o diamonds, Jack o diamonds don't lie. If I don't get my whisky, I'll drink til I die." Had I got the words right?

Sometimes I was back in the tent at South Tonchan. Cholera was still raging. There were more empty spaces. My turn was getting near.

Next day I had a visit from Charley Hill. He had attended the same school as Jack Baldridge and I. He had a sad tale to tell and when I felt strong enough to walk, he took me to the graveyard. The names on the crosses shocked me. There were so many of my friends. Billy Young and I had sat together in the church choir for several years. He was a blonde haired, good looking lad and a fine sportsman with a good left foot. Now here he lay in this God forsaken corner of the world. I felt bitter. How would his mother and blind father take such tragic news? They would be devastated.

Padre Thorpe had moved with us and he sought me out and asked me to meet him on the hillside for church service. Looking back, I wonder how we ever kept appointments. So very few people had watches, most had been sold to buy food. That Sunday we sat on the hillside in the evening sunlight and he asked me to play Hawaiian songs as a prelude to the sermon.

That was the last time I was to see Padre Harry Thorpe until he visited the UK after the war. He came to the Yasume Club at South Shields and we had a laugh when I reminded him of "Hot sweet coffee" at South Tonchan.

Many years later I met Mr Wally Kirly and his wife Mavis. They hailed from

Cootamundra, the birthplace of Don Bradman. In conversation, I mentioned Padre Thorpe. "He was my Sunday School teacher," said Mavis (small world!).

I was soon on the track again. We were working on a cutting which was through rock. Some of the rocks were easy enough to break and we put the pieces in baskets and got rid of them in the jungle. But with others there was not a single crack or flaw into which we could strike our picks. Hammers just bounced off.

It was decided that we would have to try heat and cold. We collected wood and started a huge fire on the rock. We then collected water from the river; this was to be thrown on when the rock was hot.

It was an extremely hot day and always hotter in rock cuttings, but working with fire must have been too much for me: some of the water collected for the rock had to be thrown on me!

On 18 August 1943, I moved from Tonchan to Tarso.

CHAPTER 9

Tha Soe (Tarso)

 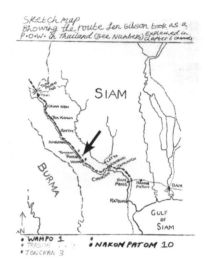

My return to Tarso was memorable due to a remarkable coincidence. Ernie Maughan, Wilf White and I had become good friends right from the TA days. We'd been like the three musketeers and gone everywhere right until the Japs parted us. I arrived in Tarso not knowing a soul and on the first morning, I wandered out onto the clearing and sat on a tree stump. I'd lost a lot of weight and by then had a thick red beard and thought I'd be unrecognisable. Suddenly, Wilf White walked up to me and said: "Hi Len." We had a lot to say to each other and when I complained about my beard, he offered to get rid of it for me.

He produced a tiny pair of scissors and proceeded to clip away very patiently. I was thinking of what a coincidence it was when a skeleton-like figure walked very unsteadily up to us and said: "Hi Len, Hi Wilf." For a while we did not recognise him. Ernie was always a big, well-made lad, weighing in at around twelve stones. He was now reduced to about five stones and showing every bone through his skin. I don't think he was able to walk very much but seeing us had been a spur. We had much to tell each other before Ernie had to get back to his hospital hut. It would be a long time before he would be fit again.

When I thought of all the places we'd been as a trio and now the three of us meeting in such a place and under such circumstances, it was an amazing coincidence.

Wilf and I managed to get on the same working party but after only two weeks, I went down with another malaria attack. I began to feel that my left side was sore and resorted to sleeping on my right. My hip became very red and swollen and

64

developed into a large abscess. The doctor said it would have to be lanced when I was over the malaria.

At the appointed time, I reported to the doctor's hut and found myself in the company of six others with exactly the same complaint. In front of me in the queue was a young Australian lad. The patient ahead of him climbed onto the makeshift table and the doctor made one deft stoke with his knife. That was enough for the young Aussie: he was off like a shot and I did not see him again!

To this day, I have a three-inch scar to remind me of the occasion.

The cut took a long time to mend as there were no healing salves and things became worse when a second one began to develop on my right buttock. I was forced to try and sleep on my front and on the bamboo slats that was extremely uncomfortable.

I was put into a hospital hut and did not like it at all. There were no facilities and nothing to distinguish it from an ordinary working hut, but I suppose the medics could keep an eye on us better. Halfway down there was a bit of a screen and beyond this were the sick officers. Their conditions differed little from ours. Officers passed to and fro. One was a tall, slim, refined looking captain wearing a Lanarkshire Yeomanry badge in his cap. We were later to become good friends.

Wilf

Wilf called to see me and drew my attention to a small sore on his leg. It was only about an inch in diameter. He wondered if it was worthy of a visit to the MO. A few days' later, that sore had spread and Wilf was having treatment. He was reluctant to go into the ulcer ward: they were truly awful places.

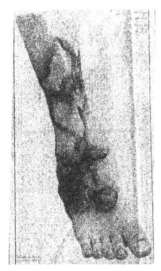

The stench alone was nauseating. Men were lying there with large open sores and in many of these were maggots, placed there by medics to eat away the rotten flesh. Teddy Minto was there and most of the bones in his ankle were visible. Other men were showing large sections of their shinbones as the ulcers stretched from just below the knee down to their feet. As there were no bandages, pieces of cloth were boiled in old petrol cans and used over and over again.

Sadly, Wilf did end up in one of these wards and I visited him regularly hoping to see some improvement, but

Horror: Tropical ulcers.

65

every time I noticed the ulcer getting larger. A day came when Wilf was in tears as he told me that the leg must be amputated. I tried to cheer him up, but he could not bear the thought of going home a cripple.

On 17 October 1943, I went with the stretcher party taking him to the operating hut. I sat on the ground outside until he was brought out, then followed them to see him settled in a bed space. The medical orderlies convinced me there was nothing I could do and assured me that they would let me know of any change.

Wilf lay all the next day without opening his eyes or responding to my voice, but early next day an orderly asked me to come urgently. I feared the worst and was just in time to hear a few words before he died. He had a small brown plastic cross in his hand and asked me to give it to his mother. I could not believe it: Wilf dead; Wilf who could not hurt a fly; Wilf who was so gentle and so naïve. Next day, 20 October, we buried him. It was a day of despair.

I could not believe that Wilf was gone. We'd only met up a few weeks ago and he was fitter than any of us. Now I'd never see him again. I was losing so many of my close friends. I could not bear to stay in the hut and spent most of the time in the jungle as I was no fit company for anyone. Until it became too dark, I only returned for meals.

I did not speak to a soul in that dreadful hut, but where things were made worse was when one poor man cried all night and called out loudly for his friend who had just been buried. I hated being awake at night as there were no sides to the hut which was near to the gateway leading to the graveyard, and one could not ignore the sad succession of medical orderlies carrying the latest victims of Japanese inhumanity to man (all these ulcers were curable, but the Japs would not, or could not be bothered to supply our MOs with the necessary ointments). I had a temperature the next day and hid myself under a piece of old mosquito net. I only stirred when a voice asked me how I was and if I would be playing my guitar. It was the Lanarkshire Yeomanry Captain. I explained that I had just lost my best friend and he was most sympathetic.

(In 1957 I was to receive a letter from America in which the Captain stated that he was writing his memoirs and had reached a point where he was awakened out of a coma by me playing my guitar.) Evidently, he must have been just on the other side of that screen.

Meanwhile, that second abscess on my buttock was getting worse. In fact, it became enormous and I had to pay a second visit to the "knife man". The outcome was more serious. Instead of healing, it spread, and a hole developed. From then on, I had to have daily treatment.

An orderly made a ball of material about the size of a tennis ball, dipped it in "aqua-flavine" which was the only thing available, and inserted it into the hole. There were no bandages as such, and I tore up what was left of my one and only shirt so that I could wrap it round my waist and hide the two wounds. I must have presented a pretty awful sight!

For weeks I did not have a full night's sleep, and even sitting down was a problem. It was a miracle that the wounds finally healed up. I thought of the tiny ulcers I'd seen which eventually caused men to die and for some unknown reason I was spared. What a blessing it was when I could sleep normally again.

That particular pleasure was short lived. Another abscess developed just about three inches from where the second one had recently healed, so for the third time I had to visit the "knife man". Sadly, the result was the same. Another big hole was left and had to be treated similarly to the last. If anything, this was even bigger and it was necessary to lie on my front once again. Whilst attending the ulcer hut for attention, I would often see a person carefully painting pictures of the most serious ulcers. That person I met later and he was Jack Chalker. As cameras were forbidden, his paintings would be a valuable record.

So, my first few months at Tha Soe (Tarso) had not been happy ones. I'd had four attacks of malaria, three abscesses and the sadness of Wilf's death before I could return to the main camp. For the next few months, it was work with the Jap guards and more bullying. Sometimes we were building huts, sometimes digging trenches, sometimes pile driving and sometimes water carrying for the cookhouses.

Not having met up with any of my regiment, I was working with men I did not know, but we were all in the same boat as it were and all got on well together. Going out on one particular party, I was partnering someone I'd never seen before. We'd walked a long way from camp and were passing through a Thai settlement. It was a small clearing with one large bamboo hut on stilts.

There were several hens scratting around and this interested my friend. He asked me if I liked chicken. Without waiting for an answer, he held me back and let the rest of the column follow the Jap. He nodded in the direction of one bird and gave me a knowing wink. With knees well bent and nearly touching the ground, we herded the hen off the track and towards the jungle.

My friend then made a sudden grab and had the bird. I asked him what he was going to do next. We could not take it with us. He said he would hypnotise it and pick it on the way back. I began to think I had met a loony. What he did next amazed me: holding the bird by its neck in his left hand, he pressed it to the ground and with the forefinger of his right hand he drew a line in the dust across the front of its beak.

We had to hurry to catch up with the others, but I looked back once or twice and the creature had not moved a feather. My comrade told me not to worry as it would still be there when we returned. Unfortunately, at the end of the day, the Jap brought us back by a different route so I never got to know if the hypnotic trance lasted, and I never got to know the taste of that Thai chicken.

There were wild fowl living in the jungle and although I often heard them and sometimes even saw them, they were impossible to catch by hand as they lived in thick, thorny undergrowth. It was extremely frustrating to be so near to them and unable to reach them.

I was delighted when a group of our original work battalion came down from up country. Many of my regiment and some of my close friends were among them: Michael Conlin, Charley Carney, Jack Baldridge, Tammy Cambleman and Zalo Susarte were all in the Wampo entertainment party, so it was like old times.

Of course, they were here to work and although the railway track was completed, the Japs still continued their brutal treatment. Jack Baldridge and I were put in a work party and taken to a place I think was Tardan. The whole atmosphere in this place was strange. The guards seemed miserable and tense. We wondered if they'd had bad news.

Had their army suffered a defeat, or were their battleships sunk. They were certainly miserable and the order went out that there was to be no singing, no music and no talking in groups at night.

What they were building there we did not know, but we felled trees and dug trenches. Things became even worse when one of our men was being beaten and could not keep his cool; he resisted and even hit back - one thing which we'd all learned was fatal. He was given a beating then tied up; a rope around his wrists; a rope around his ankle and a tight rope at the back joining the two.

He was then put into a wooden box and only let out for feeding a few minutes once or twice a day. The bonds were never untied. At feeding times, a guard would grab the nearest POW and force him to spoon feed the poor victim.

A POW was also ordered the odorous task of taking the poor chap to the toilet. It was pitiful to see him struggling to get to the trees. Apart from these occasions, we were not allowed to go anywhere near him. After several days a truck arrived in the camp. Shovels were put on the back and then the victim was made to hobble out to it. Two POWs were made to lift him aboard and the truck drove off. We never learned what became of the poor chap after that.

The whole camp was like a mortuary. Even Japs did not speak to each other and we had to work silently, like Zombies. Of course, there is always the chance of a lapse of memory. Twelve of us were working in a long trench and one of the group forgot and whistled a few notes before he checked himself. The guards went mad. We were all ordered out of the trench and lined up with shovels above our heads. One demented guard then went along behind us yelling and beating the backs of our legs with his cane. I was next to Jack - we had been to school together. "Getting the cane wasn't like this at West Park," he whispered.

We were very careful not to sing or whistle after that and if anyone of us was even not looking miserable, he was reminded of the consequences.

Typhus

I woke up in a strange hut and among people I did not know. My head ached and I was extremely hot. I was informed that my friends had brought me in. The friends must have been Michael and Charley for I vaguely remember working with them and starting to feel very drowsy. Apart from giving me that piece of information, I was left to myself. This wasn't my usual malaria; I had nearly twenty of those and this was worse. The next morning an orderly took my temperature: it was 102 (I was surprised that the camp had a thermometer). The chap next to me was an Aussie and his temperature was also 102. All day my head ached and burned.

Next morning the orderly took my temperature and it was 103. The Aussie next to me was also 103. All day my head ached and burned. The next day the orderly took my temperature and it was 104. The Ausssie's was also 104. My head continued to ache and I longed to be in the cool river.

After six days I was feeling hungry and despite my headache, I wanted to eat but I was informed that I had typhus and had to be starved.

My pals came to see me and when they asked me how I was, I made the mistake of saying, "Couldn't be worse." I have resolved never to say that phrase again – because things can be worse!

Hardly had they departed, it was nearly dark, when two scorpions which were fighting in the atap roof fell upon my bare chest. Instead of stinging each other, they stung me. I staggered down to the orderly at the end of the hut and by the light of an oil lamp, he showed up four small marks and painted my chest purple. He apologised that he could do no more but advised me not to lie down or I might die. Where he had learned his medicine I do not know, but I took him at his word and resolved to stay on my feet. My chest started to thump, thump, thump and my head started to thump, thump, thump, and then my whole body started to thump, thump, thump. It was moonlight and I wandered up and down the hut and round and round the hut, then did the same thing in reverse. I picked up my guitar and tried to take my mind off the thumping and the pain, but it seemed at times that I was about to explode. All night long I prayed for the dawn and all night long I resented those sleeping forms who were unaware of my plight. I longed to lie down but resisted. My legs were giving in but I staggered on. Please hurry the dawn!

This must have been the longest night of my life. I continued to stagger on and sometimes rest by holding on to the upright bamboo at the end of the hut. On one such rest I noticed one other person astir: he was creeping rather furtively which aroused my suspicion. He made his way down my hut and picked something up.

He was not aware that anyone else was awake until I stopped him and saw in his hand a mess tin. Possessions were so scarce after two years of captivity that even mess tins were a valuable commodity which could be resold.

When I accosted him he tamely handed over the booty and I returned it to the unsuspecting owner who seemed annoyed to be awakened. The whole incident lasted only about ten minutes and I was left again to my wanderings.

The night went on as did the thumpings in my body and head. At last it turned light and I was pleased to see other people on the move. I still continued to walk but it was more pleasant than in the dark. I could wander into the jungle for a change, but although my mind was willing my flesh was weak. I finally arrived at my bed space which, although it was only bamboo slats, looked so inviting. I just fell on them. If I must die, then so be it. I had done my utmost. I still could not sleep because of the thumping, but was content to enjoy the luxury of not being on my feet.

"Bombardier Gibson! Bombardier Gibson!"

Someone was calling my name from the end of the hut.

"Here," I called as loudly as I could.

"Come on lad, get your guitar. We are entertaining the sick this afternoon."

It was the Sergeant Major in charge of entertainments. I don't know how I managed but I wandered round with the concert party. They were doing *Let the people sing.* I did it as in a dream.

Next morning, the orderly took my temperature: it was 101 (an age I reached in 2021). The orderly took the Aussie's, it was 102. Without moving his head, he said: "Beat you, you pommy bastard." These are the only words he ever spoke during our ten days together. I knew then that we were friends.

I had not eaten for so long that I insisted I see the doctor. He put me on E diet. From early morning I eagerly awaited this diet. Men were given A diet, later given B diet. By afternoon some were given C diet. I was ravenous. D diet was distributed at dusk and my patience was at breaking point. At last, E diet! "Here," I shouted. What a disappointment when I was handed one small biscuit made from ground rice.

River Boat

The Japanese needed us to work down river and as there was a barge available, they must have decided that it was quicker than walking through the jungle. Nearly thirty of us were crowded into the craft, together with two guards and the Thai boatman and his wife. She was seated at the rear of the boat and he was in the bow with a long pole.

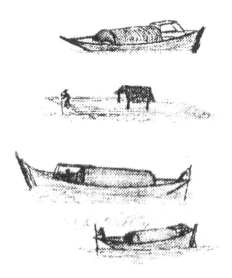

I did not like the look of the river. It was flowing extremely quickly and the Thai woman looked too frail to steer the laden craft. The Thai poled us away from the bank and soon we were in midstream. I wished we had been going up river for soon we were going down with the flow at a very fast pace. The Thai and his wife were continually shouting at each other and, although we could not understand their words, their demeanour caused us some anxiety. We gathered such speed as to cause alarm, then when the Thais became more agitated and their shouts more urgent, we realised that the barge was out of control.

We were now going at break-neck speed and ahead of us was a bend. At times we were at an angle despite the efforts of the steerer. We looked ahead anxiously hoping that we would be able to negotiate the bend. Then the boat started to turn. In fact, it nearly did a complete circle before crashing into the overhanging vegetation.

The next I knew I was hanging onto a bough and up to my waist in water. I looked around and saw two or three more clinging to the trees. We climbed onto higher boughs to be clear of the water and watched the barge disappear round the bend. We had no idea how long it would be before it could get back to pick us up, or if it would be back before dark. It was imperative that we stayed put so that we could be found. We had to be patient. Luckily, the trees sheltered us from the sun, and the heat soon dried us out. The hours passed and we were tired of scanning the river for a boat; any boat so long as we did not have to spend all night sitting up a tree.

One of the others was a sergeant: he had a dark pointed beard and still had an army issue khaki shirt. From his breast pocket, he produced a whistle. I was surprised that anyone would still carry such an article. It was with immense relief that we heard the now familiar noise of a river barge: it turned out to be ours.

What a time it had taken to regain control and get back to us. The sergeant blew his whistle loudly and guided it in. With great difficulty, we reached the boat for I had to be waist deep again and the current was dragging me down stream. I was happy to be pulled unceremoniously aboard by willing hands.

It was dark when we finally pulled into the shore and followed the guards into the jungle. We were extremely hungry but were told that there would be no MESHI until morning. There were no huts so I found a place to settle. I could not sleep and lay watching the flying foxes. These huge bats looked so ungainly as they hopped up the tree trunks yet glided so gracefully across the clearing above our heads.

I spent a most uncomfortable night and was glad to see the dawn. A group of POWs appeared with rice and tea, and then we were hustled through the jungle to where a scene of great activity met our gaze. There were huge props with pulleys and great weights hanging from them. There were long lines of bedraggled POWs pulling on long ropes while Jap guards shouted and bullied. We were now on Pile Driving: this was another monotonous and tiring job. All day we hauled on those ropes, let them go, ran to retrieve them and then hauled again. My hands were hardened by digging and shovelling but soon they were tender and sore. I was not the only sufferer for next day most of the lads had managed to find a piece of rice sack to wrap round the rope.

Time and time again we hauled on that rope; heard the Jap shout: "Ichi Ni San Ho," watched that huge blob of metal thump down onto the pile, then wearily pick up that rope again. I could not help but marvel at how they had assembled those huge tripods and fixed up those pulleys and weights. How would they move them for the next pile? As it turned out I did not last long enough to see for after a few days I was hit by another attack of malaria. I became so hot and feverish that I could hardly see the weight falling but heard the thump as it struck. I longed for water. I longed for the end of the day when I could submerge myself in the river.

There were some containers lying there from morning meal and I imagined that there might be some cold tea or water in one of them. Throwing caution to the wind, I hurried over to look but was disappointed. Unfortunately, I had been spotted by one of the guards. He came running at me shouting, and before I could get back to the rope, he hit me with the stick he was carrying. He caught me on the side of my head near my left eye, and for some time I must have been dazed for I felt hands grabbing me and guiding me back to the rope.

By the end of the next day the whole of the side of my face was black and blue and my left eye closed up. With that and the malaria, I was in a sorry state and the Japs sent me back to Tarsoa with a group of sick and injured.

It took a long time for my face to heal and years later when free and back home, my mother said: "What did they do to your eye?" and as she said that she touched the very spot where the Jap had hit me.

CHAPTER 10

Nakom Pathon

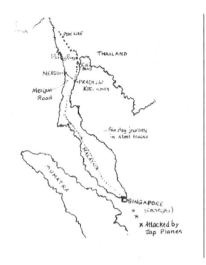

On 20 April 1944, just as I was starting another dose of malaria, we received orders to move. Rumour had it that we were going down country: that was good news. The second piece of information was that we were travelling by train: this rather alarmed me. I wondered if I would not prefer to walk. I remembered all the little acts of sabotage we had perpetrated and imagined the train coming off the line.

We had to assemble with our belongings to walk to the station. Belongings? I was not overburdened. To wear, I had only a ragged pair of shorts (no shirt, no boots, no hat). Apart from a mess tin with a bent spoon, an old ground sheet and a piece of mosquito net, I had my guitar. Inside this I carried my old pay book and a shorthand dictionary and diary.

Crowded as we were, I did enjoy the journey and we alighted at a place called 'Nong Pladuk'. Because of the fever, I saw little of that place and two days later arrived at Nakom Pathom. I have no recollection of how I got there. Was it by train or did I walk there in a trance?

Nakom Pathon was in the plains of Thailand. What a change to be out of the jungle! What a pleasant change to be able to look into the distance! One distant object was very prominent: it was the temple of Nakom Pathon city. It was a Wat and shone like gold in the sunlight.

The huts were much improved on those up country. They were framed with wood not bamboo, but still had atap roofs. They were large; each one holding about a hundred men. We'd slept on bamboo slats when up country so flat boards were a luxury. There were British, Australian, Dutch and Americans in camp.

There was an enclosure for the mentally disturbed. There was also a pretty stagnant pond. Work was varied. Sometimes, we would be digging a huge trench around the camp and sometimes working in the fields.

We cleared a huge area and planted it with cotton. Rumour had it that the Japanese CO was in the cotton trade back home in Japan. Twice I went out with barrow parties and when nearing Nakom Pathon city, I hoped that we may pass close enough to find out what the Temple was like close up. We saw neat little houses on stilts: they were the homes of the priests.

In our hut, only Billy McCready and I were from our regiment. We'd been there for a few weeks when I had a visit from an officer who said his name was Norman Smith. He explained that he was forming an orchestra and wondered if I would be interested. I was delighted and turned up at the first rehearsal. Norman was a great musician and had a good voice. Our signature tune was *The Melody Maker*. He always sang it.

We played a wide variety of music ranging from: Bounce Me Brother to a Solid Four to Die Fledermaus. The violinists were Captain Wilson, Eskes and Sanderson. The clarinettist was Captain Martin of the East Surrey Regiment. The two trumpeters were a Russian named Tebneff and an Australian. A Javanese called Jimmy Van Lingden played guitar and there was a banjo player known to all as Sinbad.

I remember playing Night and Day, El Relicario, Torna a Sorriento, Paggliacci, Hungarian Dances and Tales from the Vienna Woods, and many more pieces which I liked.

Norman Smith was a Fellow of the Royal College of Organists. He was also a fully Chartered Accountant; a good rugby player; a good cricketer and no one could beat him at card games of skill. He also had a terrific memory for music; he was a true all rounder.

Playing in the band was a challenge. I had taught myself the chords and this was the test. We gave regular concerts playing to large audiences. There was a good tenor who sang semi classical songs and we had solos from different members of the orchestra. Eskes was a huge Dutchman who had broadcast and most of the others were professional musicians who had played in well-known orchestras. Tebneff had been a cadet in the White Russian Army. He had played in a band, and when driven out during the revolution had had to resort to playing for a living in Hong Kong. He became a British citizen.

Jimmy Van Lingden was a good guitarist with an excellent ear for chords. He was a small man and had a huge homemade guitar which he handled with expertise.

Sinbad was really Petty Officer Alec Hawes. He had a dark beard and always reminded me of the sailor on the front of the old Players cigarette packet.

Apart from the orchestra, there was a first-class comedy duo: Captain Fisser Pearson and Eric Griffiths-Jones provided hours of laughter. It all served to take our minds off the Japanese.

A Fiddler Called Jameson

We'd just been dismissed after a hard day's work when he came to me and said: "Are you the chap who has a guitar?" When I replied in the affirmative, he went on: "I can borrow a fiddle for tonight. Do you fancy a session? I'll come round to your hut tonight after mishi (food)."

He duly arrived that night and I learned that his name was Jameson and that he'd played at barn dances in Northumberland. I'd invited my Aussie friend Sinbad to join us. He arrived with his banjo and the three of us started up with a medley of North Country tunes including Blaydon Races and Keep Your Feet Still Geordie Hinnie. We immediately drew a crowd.

There were about a hundred POWs in our hut and a hundred in the huts on either side. Soon all three hundred seemed to be converging upon us. At one stage I looked up and realised that some were on the roof and had lifted up the atap tiles so as to be able to see. What a singsong! What a wealth of willing talent kept the concert going and Jameson was never at a loss to fill in the gaps. The singalong was a great success. In fact, too much of a success and too loud. We failed to hear lights out and continued our raucous singing for an hour or so after. The Japs must have had enough: they called out the guard and with fixed bayonets charged.

What a scatter there was!

The noise was like a stampede of cattle as men ran to the shelter of their own places. Jameson and I were caught and marched to the guardhouse. There we were interrogated, slapped, interrogated again then made to stand outside the guardroom with our instruments held above our heads. They could not comprehend how two quiet instruments could be the cause of so much noise. They wanted to know of "other man" but we insisted that there was no other. My pal Sinbad had escaped and we weren't going to tell. Our arms ached and our heads were sore through taking the weight of the instruments.

Just before dawn we were allowed to go. That was the last time I saw Jameson – well, so I thought at the time.

It was 1947 and war and prisoner of war camps were completely out of my mind. I was studying hard now, training to be a teacher, and to add to my worries, I was a married man and my wife was expecting our first child. Yes, I had survived six years of war, three-and-a-half years of hell in a prisoner of war camp and now was settled down to be a civilian. I was training at a college near Preston, and a weekend free was not only a luxury from bookwork, but an opportunity to get home to Sunderland to see my wife.

On a cold November night, I set off from Preston by train and had to change at Carlisle. What a bleak place that station was just after the war. The rain was sleeting down and shelter was non-existent. Cold, wet and miserable, I found myself the only person on the platform. I was beginning to wonder if I'd got my train times correct when one other person appeared at the other end of the platform. How pleased I was to see another human. I plucked up the courage to approach him to ask if he knew what time the train was due.

As I walked up to him, he also took steps in my direction. "Gibson!" he almost yelled. I could hardly believe my ears or my eyes.

"Jameson," I replied.

"The same," said he as we warmly shook hands and started to question each other about what we were doing in such a place and at such an hour. The train eventually arrived and having settled down in an empty compartment, we never stopped talking until all too soon we arrived at his destination. He alighted and I watched him disappear in the dim light of the station. Only when he was out of sight I remembered that we had not posed the vital questions that would have kept us in touch: address. I didn't even know his first name.

And so Jameson, the fiddler, went out of my life but never out of my mind for I often have pleasure in recalling the two brief encounters we had all those many years ago.

Colonel (Weary) Dunlop

Having had over twenty doses of malaria, dysentery, typhus, ulcers and beri-beri, I started to experience a pain which was totally different. What now? Billy McCready called an orderly and in due course Captain McConochie examined me and announced that I must have my appendix out.

Next morning I was taken to the "theatre". I say "theatre" but I have seen many better garden sheds on allotment sites. Colonel Dunlop was there and I was given an injection in my spine. When I felt the knife, I sat up supported on my elbows to have a look. I should have remained silent but when I saw just a worm of blood above the cut, I said: "There's not much blood!" (I'd expected blood to gush out from the wound.)

Colonel Dunlop turned to an orderly standing by and said: "Put his shoulders down and keep him quiet." The orderly complied and after a while whispered to me:"Where do you come from?" "Sunderland," I replied. "So do I," said he. "Which part?" "Millfield," I replied. "So do I," said he. "Which street?"

We discovered that we lived in the next street to each other and were meeting for the very first time on the other side of the world. He was a Bombardier like me but was in the 135 field regiment. He had been a semi-professional boxer in Civvy Street.

(A few years after the war, I was invited to join the Fellowship of the Services. I reported to the upstairs room of the *George and Dragon* and on duty at the door was none other than Bombardier Brown who had held me down.) We both became Chairmen of the Fellowship and for many years met every Thursday afternoon with a group of POWs.

The night of the operation, I was put in a different hut. I lay on my old ground sheet and wrapped myself up in my piece of mosquito net until I was like a mummy. I awoke in the middle of the night hearing someone saying: "That man must be made of iron."

As he was the only other person around, I presumed he was referring to me. The speaker was sitting on a metal box in the centre aisle. Only one other man was in the hut because he could not walk.

Colonel (Weary) Dunlop.

By the light of a little oil lamp, he was killing bugs and counting 563, 564, 565, 566.

I quickly arose and joined the hundreds of others who were sleeping out in the open. The Japs objected to this, but our lads would not go back to be eaten alive by bugs. Less than 24 hours after the operation, I was working. All the floorboards had to be levered up and taken out to bonfires. Every piece of timber had to be passed through the flames in order to burn all the bugs and their eggs.

In the scorching hot sun, plus the heat from the fires, I sweated. There was no such thing as sticking plaster, and it was difficult to keep my wound covered. I would now have four scars to remind me of prison life, but luckily they would all be covered by a pair of swimming trunks.

That night Teb called to see me. We called him Teb, but his full name was Nicholai Phillippe Tebneff. With fellow escaping Russian cadets, he had formed a band and as well as playing in cities like Shanghai and Hong Kong, had toured Japan. He had picked up some of the Nippon language and at South Wampo acted as interpreter.

After the Japs gave him a severe beating, he swore never to speak Nipponese again. He had a wife and children but had had the foresight to get them out of Malaya before the invasion. They were then in India.

As we were both involved with the band, he suggested that I move to the hut with other musicians. This proved to be a splendid arrangement. I could pick the brains of the others and learn a little of their instruments.

At Wampo I had experimented with chords and rhythms trying to describe the coming of the rainy season. I was fascinated by the changes in the creatures of the forest; how they sensed the coming of the rain; how the gentle breeze cooled us before lashing us with the torrent it carried.

Sitting round the campfire the lads would often ask me to play Jungle. I decided to rename it Monsoon and write it as an orchestral piece. Before Norman Smith arrived at rehearsals, I would take the opportunity to put a piece in front of some of the band and ask if they would play it to see what it sounded like. In time, I had the orchestration complete.

It was with great trepidation that I handed out parts to unsuspecting players and had the temerity to say: "Please come in after the count of four." I was not only the youngest, but also the only amateur, but the band responded really well.

Norman Smith had heard the whole thing but kept out of the way until it was finished. He not only approved but rewrote all the band parts on good paper. At the next concert, Monsoon was included in the programme and at the end, Norman made me take a bow. I learned that when Norman Smooth was moved with the officers to another camp, he still played Monsoon with newly formed bands.

As Christmas approached, the Padre asked me to join a choir. I found myself in illustrious company: there was Major E W Swanton (sportswriter and later author of many books on cricket, including the life of Denis Compton); Captain Lawrence Turner (owner of a chemical factory and later to become MP for Oxford); Captain David Ffolkes (Architect and stage and film designer – involved later in some Bond films).

Apart from practising carols, I was asked to assist Captain Ffolkes to make the bare hut more Christmassy. The Captain decided to create a nativity scene but in Medieval costume. He was also Officer in charge of the Convalescent Block. He and Captain Turner were in the next hut to Teb and I would often stop and chat as they passed through.

Captain Ffolkes was well used to making models for stage productions and with very little help from me he soon had a most unusual but attractive nativity scene. It really looked great but certain traditionalists did not approve. On Christmas Day and for the carol service, he lit little candles to set it off. Sadly, in the middle of the service, the whole thing caught fire.

So, I worked for the Japs by day and tried to forget them by night through involving myself in things musical. There were now a number of our regiment in Nakom Pathon and we got together for a chat on New Year's Eve. John Glancy and Eddy Kent were both pianists and were interested in my involvement with the camp band. They attended rehearsals as well as concerts and with their keen ears for music could name the notes and the chords which we were playing.

Sergeant Ted Minto heard me sing J'attendrais and insisted that I teach it to him. Jock Aird, Tommy Old, John Sugden, Jack Robinson, Bill McCready and Pat Geldart often gathered for a chat.

Three days after New Year's Day was my birthday (my third in captivity) and I don't know how they found out, but both Lawrence Turner and Captain Ffolkes gave me cards. One was painted by Jack Chalker and showed me in my jap happy playing my guitar on one side and dressed in tails conducting an orchestra on the other.

Painted by Jack Chalker and given to me by David Ffolkes.

The other showed British Soldiers in Spain listening to a guitar during the Peninsula War. Considering our situation, I was amazed that anyone was still able to acquire paper and paints; I still treasure these.

Jack Chalker was the artist I used to see painting ulcers at Tarsoa. Some years later, I had the good fortune to meet up with him. He and his wife, and my wife and I, spent a great evening together.

New Year card drawn by Jack Chalker (now a successful artist) showing Len Gibson playing his guitar and wearing his "Jap Happy".

Reunion: Len with his wife Ruby (left) and Jack Chalker and his wife (right).

In Nakom Pathon camp there was a POW camp inside a POW camp. In this inner compound were Indian soldiers who had remained loyal to Britain. Thousands of other Indians had defected to the Japanese, but this group had remained faithful despite a great deal of PRESSURE(?) from our captors.

The Japanese did not allow any contact between us and those gallant Indians, but seven of us managed to get inside their compound. Eddy Kent from my regiment, Paddy Cusack - a great Irish lad, Browny – a lad from Derbyshire, Coley - an Aussie who was a bass player and had permanent rhythm, and myself were very fond of singing in harmony. We practised together and called ourselves "5 boys and 6 strings".

The Japs would not allow the band or concert party into the Indian Compound but listened to us and decided we could do no harm. We had a British Officer who was in the Indian army and was anxious to contact the Indians, and so he became one of our group just for the occasion. A Jap guard marched us in and found all the Indians seated on the ground and waiting our arrival.

It was ludicrous. These poor Indians most of whom could speak no English sat while we sang such songs as The Boogy Woogy Bugle Boy from Company B. As we sang the English Officer sat beside an Indian CO and talked urgently and exchanged much information. At the end the Indian Captain made a vote of thanks which lasted three times as long as our programme. In the end, the Jap guard could stand no more and marched us out.

There was another compound inside the camp. It contained one solitary soul: he was a leper. My attacks of malaria were not so frequent since we had moved out of the jungle, but I was still troubled by a large rash which appeared on my chest and on my buttocks: this rash was extremely itchy.

Another cause for concern was when my left arm became useless. I just could not raise it at all. At the same time, I had a constant pain on the top of the shoulder. I was given daily massage by a medic who had spent a lot of time in boxing gyms. It was several weeks before I could return to playing my guitar. The Jap guards could see nothing wrong with my arm and expected me to work as usual.

The Japanese Camp Commandant ordered all POWs to do exercises and it was to be done to music. Norman Smith was given an eight bar Nipponese tune and the band had to play this over and over again. A Dutch POW, an ex-school teacher, led these exercises from the top of a raised platform.

CHAPTER 11

The Mergui Road

Nakom Pathon in Thailand: 12 April 1945

A few hundred starved and nearly naked prisoners standing in long rows while fully dressed Japanese guards search through the pathetic belongings which the prisoners had laid out in front of them.

The question they were all asking themselves: "Where to and what to do?" These men had been in similar situations before and on one occasion, they'd ended up slaving to build a railway – a railway of death – for 16,000 of their comrades had died in its construction.

Harsh conditions; starvation diet; lack of medical supplies; malaria; dysentery; beri-beri; cholera; typhus - they'd suffered it all and it showed in their bodies and faces.

The irony of it all, they had now been chosen as fit for another such task.

Little did any of them know at the time, but this was going to be even worse. More than three out of every five of them would be dead within four months.

The sun was up and the heat was almost unbearable when we finally marched off (I say WE), because I with three others from my regiment, was ONE MORE FOR THE ROAD.

We walked towards the railway station and were pleased to be allocated to open goods trucks.

In his book "Comrades in Bondage", Frank Foster headed the chapter on the Mergui Road, "Worse than the Railway." I agree!

We had all suffered the experience of being packed, nearly forty, in a closed steel truck for five days and nights on a journey from Singapore to Thailand. However, we soon began to have reservations for the engines were fuelled by logs and burning embers showered upon our bare torsos. An outburst of rain was a blessed relief.

The journey was extremely uncomfortable.

At one stage we had to alight and carry assorted equipment along the track. We were amazed to find ahead of us a bridge with no middle! Had our RAF or Navy been responsible? We cherished the thought.

The Japs had constructed a rough bridgeway with timbers and to get to the other side we were to WALK THE PLANK.

The planks were narrow and the drop to the river some fifty feet. We observed that there was little water, the riverbed mainly being covered with rocks and sand.

When my turn came, I was given a small but heavy crate, and I stepped onto the planks behind another poor POW who was struggling with a kwali on his head. It was like being on a tightrope, and for anyone scared of heights, it was a nightmare. I inched forward not daring to look down, then suddenly the man with a kwali on his head stopped dead in his tracks. Despite shouts from both POWs and Japs, he would not move. We could not go forward and it was impossible to turn around and go back.

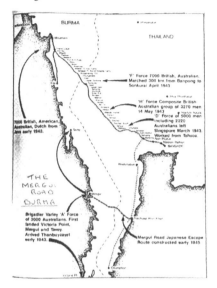

There was more shouting and more threats. I stood there praying that he would move. Suddenly, he dropped to his knees to grab the planks with both hands. Of course, the kwali fell from his head. I watched it sway from side to side before crashing on the rocks below. I had to be really unkind and threaten to kick him off if he did not go forward.

When we finally reached the other side, the enraged Japs forced the unfortunate chap to descend to the riverbed to retrieve a piece of the metal. I suppose this was to appease their quartermaster.

To our dismay we had to go back for a second load. On the first trip I had had my guitar slung across my back and I thought the second time would be easier without it. However, it was still a nightmare and I was relieved to reach the other side again and be reunited with my guitar. I think the Japs referred to that particular place as Ratburi, but that was not to be our destination. After a brief rest, it was "All men go" and we were on the move again.

We reached a place named Kirrikan and began a long walk into the interior. The guards bullied the stragglers and urged the column for greater speed. Several times planes were heard overhead and the Japs seemed very concerned and herded us under trees. We had not seen our captors show such anxiety before and it pleased us to know that at least we had allied planes in the area.

At one stage when they allowed a rest, we discovered that most of us had blood around our toes. Further examination revealed the cause: we'd been picking up leeches and some were still nestling between our toes. Salt or burning cigarettes usually caused them to drop off, but we knew that to pull them might mean that they could leave their heads inside us. As salt and cigarettes were not always readily available, we learned the trick of wetting our thumbs with our saliva and stroking the heads of these detestable bloodsuckers. From then on we made regular checks on each other's legs and feet.

We were glad to see the back of it.

Our journey continued and occasionally we met the odd person coming from up country, and what a sorry sight they were. Some had appalling ulcers, unbandaged and covered with flies and they walked like zombies. The misery in their eyes warned us of what lay in store for us.

From then on we hardly spoke to each other: we feared the worst.

The tension was broken by of all things, a dog. It suddenly appeared from the jungle and walked along with us wagging its tail as if pleased to be in our company. Of course the lads made a fuss of it and, although the Japs chased it off, it would reappear sometime later. Because it came out of the jungle, it was decided to call it "Jungle". The Japs continued to chase it and the lads were always glad to see it return.

Sometimes, after being threatened by the guards, it would be away so long that we feared we would never see it again and then suddenly, it would be amongst us much to the disgust of the guards.

Meanwhile, the column made slow progress. Many of the POWs were still suffering the effects of dysentery and after forced stoppages were too weak to catch up. Many had malaria and staggered along in silence.

For many the effort was too much for their weak and tired legs, and there was the heat: with no breeze, it was unbearable. The Japs shouted and bullied but the men could not respond and the column stretched even longer.

We practically collapsed into the first camp and after sorting ourselves out into various primitive huts, we ate the usual bowl of rice and gippo, and then fell into a sound sleep.

Next morning we paraded for Tenko and were marched off carrying an assortment of spades and chunkels. When working on the railway, I was with B, D and F Battalion and it was our job to clear a swathe through the jungle in readiness for the tracklayers. We built embankments and hacked through hills. The work here was to be the same except that it did not require the swathe to be as straight or as level.

It became evident that we were cutting a track across the Kra Isthmus to a place in Burma called Mergui. We were not sure if it was to be a supply route or an escape route. What we did know was that, like the railway we'd built, it had previously been surveyed and deemed too costly in human lives.

What a lucky person I was to be caught up in both these deadly projects!

We soon started to lose men, some through accident, but mainly through sickness and fatigue. Many arrived and just collapsed and never managed to raise a finger to assist the Japs in the building of their cursed road.

After only a few days' work, one poor chap had the top of his scalp taken off by a falling bough. There was no help available and no hospital for hundreds of miles. To add to our misery at night we could hear his screams. We lay awake; unable to ignore his cries; aware of the hopelessness of our plight and praying some miracle might happen and we could be transported from this hellhole.

I realised that I had a tough fight on my hands. I had to stay on my feet and avoid accidents or else I would soon be dead. The food we had been given on the journey had been atrocious and if we expected better when settled in camp, we were going to be very disappointed.

In our three years of captivity, we had been offered some insipid concoctions, but nothing to compare with the food on the Mergui Road. It looked like cabbage, but was dry and brittle, so had to be soaked before it could be boiled. Hence, we called it "gas cape". Any fresh vegetables which arrived in camp went straight to the Jap cookhouse.

For several weeks the rations reached us by elephant and trouble started when one particular tusker did the run with its baby. This latter was a vicious little beast and news of its impending arrival sent alarm bells ringing through the camp. Japs disappeared into their huts and POWs scurried off into the jungle.

This little jumbo hated all humans and went charging after any it laid its eyes on,

AND it could move with speed. Mother elephant had the mahout on its neck and two baskets on its back. The supplies in these baskets had to be taken to the Jap store. The mahout refused to make the elephant kneel and would never get down from its back or assist in any way.

I sometimes wondered if he too was afraid of the baby. He just sat there waiting for someone to empty the baskets. The Japs would not, so it was left to some unfortunate POW to brave the baby jumbo and retrieve the supplies from the panniers and make a dash for the store hut.

On several occasions I was the unfortunate POW and what a cat and mouse game I had: dodging round mother; diving under its belly; grabbing pieces from the basket when I could, then running like a hare into the store hut where a Jap quickly slammed the door once I was safe inside. This went on until the baskets were empty.

It was heartbreaking to see and handle the occasional pumpkin and melon and then go back to rice and gas cape stew. There were also packages which delighted our guards and roused our imagination, but we knew that to steal any of these would be courting an early grave. In our weak condition, any punishment meted out by Japs would be final.

Men were dying from disease and malnutrition and every day bodies would be wrapped in rice sacks and placed in shallow graves. Those who were too ill to work but could be moved were sent down to camps nearer to Kirrikan. John Sugden and Jack Robinson, the two friends from my regiment departed this way, and I feared for their wellbeing.

Jungle, the dog which followed us up country, followed us into the first camp and even turned up on the first Tenko. Of course, the Japs chased it off, but it growled before leaving. In fact, it was uncanny the way it sensed the presence of any

Japanese and bared its teeth, yet wagged its tail and came to any of the prisoners.

This did not please the guards, and the next time it turned up at Tenko, they went for it with sticks. Jungle disappeared again into the undergrowth, but turned up again on parade the next day.

This time the sentries arrived with rifles at ready, but before they could take aim, Jungle was off. The Japs made it known that Jungle was wanted dead or alive and any POW sheltering it would be punished.

The Diary

As a 15 year old in my last year at school, I followed what was known as the Commercial Course and we did Pitman's Shorthand. When clearing bomb damage in Singapore, I'd found much to my delight a Pitman's Pocket Shorthand Dictionary. Searching further, I'd found a loose-leaf jotter, and from then on I'd kept notes in simple shorthand.

For three years I managed to hide these when the Japs were doing their occasional searches. Sometimes they were hidden inside my guitar; sometimes in a piece of hollow bamboo; and often in an emergency in my jap happy.

At Nakom Pathon, because of my guitar playing, I had been allowed to have paper and pencil purely for the writing of music: I still have these today. The Japanese Interpreter did not sign his name to authorise, but had his own stamp which he stuck on my manuscript.

These papers were precious to me and I had to hide them, not only from the Japs, but also from the cigarette smokers who rolled their own using locally grown tobacco. Paper was a rare commodity in the jungle and even bibles were sacrificed to the cigarette addicts. It always amazed me how clever some of the lads were at splitting paper for not only did it give them a better smoke, but doubled their stocks. Had they discovered my dictionary, it would have gone up in smoke.

I got back from work one day to find the Jap corporal sitting near my bed space. My guitar was lying out with all my papers around it: I paled. Why had he picked on me? Had he just been interested in my guitar and found the papers by chance? He began shouting in Japanese which of course I did not understand.

I picked up the paper with the Japanese Officer's stamp and showed it to him, but he was not satisfied. He was very suspicious of the dots and squiggles (my shorthand) which he'd never seen before. He shouted even louder and at any moment I expected him to strike me.

"These no good ka!" he yelled and picking up the shorthand papers he stamped out of the hut. Not until he was out of sight did I dare look to see if my pocket dictionary was still there. Thankfully, it was - still suspended under the bed slats where I'd left it.

All my notes were gone, but at least I still had all the important dates which I had written in the back of that dictionary.

Monsoons on the Mergui

I thought I had known the height of despondency when bitten by scorpions in the camp at Tarsoa, but I was to experience worse on the Mergui Road.

No matter what the conditions, work had to go on. There was never an excuse for stoppage. When the monsoons came, we worked in the rain, ate in rain, slept in rain. In fact, for weeks we were never dry.

Take for instance our camp. When we first arrived it resembled an oasis. It was a pleasant clearing in the midst of a jungle with a tiny stream running through and glistening in the sunlight. In a hut at the other side of the stream were my two friends, John and Jack Robinson, and to visit them just had to hop across this sparkling rivulet.

Within days this all changed dramatically; the sky blackened, the rains came and that tiny stream became a raging torrent. The whole valley was flooded and it became impossible to cross. To reach or leave our hut, we had to wade waist high or swim: it was ridiculous. The river ran through our huts and when we sat on our bed slats, our legs were in the water.

There were so many crowded in the one hut that we had to sleep head to tail. We were like sardines. Even to go to the toilet, we had to swim, but if it was just to make water, one knelt on the slats and let go into the torrent. Bamboo slats were always uncomfortable for sleeping on, but after three years, we accepted them. In the storm, the roof tiles were constantly being blown up and the rain drenched us. It was all so utterly ridiculous.

Monsoon and Misery

Sleep or no sleep, the work had to go on. Early morning the Japs were at the top of the ridge calling us for Tenko. Rain poured into our mess tins as we ate our breakfast, diluting our tea and cooling our rice.

We had to pick up our chunkels and spades and splash our way onto the track. After half-an-hour we reached the hillside where we had to continue the road making, AND THIS WAS MISERY.

Wearing only G strings with freezing rain pouring upon our skinny bodies, our bare feet sinking into the slippery cold mud, we would strain to dig out a scoopful of soggy clay then stagger a few yards to deposit it. The clay would not leave the shovel and had to be scraped off. Then we had to go back and do it again, and again and again.

The rains never ceased. Nor did the guards ever stop their shouting and bullying. We shivered and our bellies cried out for food. We'd not had a decent meal for three years ..

and our minds, ………… tortured to the point of insanity.

How much longer could we endure this misery? When will this cursed rain cease? Will this war ever end? How much longer can I hold out? Will I go the way of many of my friends and be wrapped in a rice sack and committed to the sodden earth? Will ANY of us survive?

"SPEEDO! SPEEDO!" yelled the Japs.

This must be hell on earth!!!

The longer it rained the smaller our workforce became. Men collapsed on site, could not find the strength to make the journey back to camp and had to be carried. Some just staggered back alone arriving long after the main party. It was pitiful to see. The next destination for these unfortunates was the hut across the river (the so called hospital) from whence very few escaped the rice sack.

Looking back I just don't know how I escaped the fevers and diseases which were affecting my comrades. To date, as a POW I'd had nearly thirty attacks of malaria as well as dysentery, beri-beri, typhus and tropical ulcers, so I thought that I would have been one of the first to fall foul of the terrible conditions on the Mergui Road.

I was now under six stones in weight; all my ribs were very evident; my arms and legs were painfully thin and covered with cuts and scratches; my feet were in a really bad state, and my toes were hardly visible for sores.

Despite this, I never once reported sick and never had the opportunity to miss a day's work on the road. Men dropped around me but, amazingly, I stayed on my feet. From time to time, however, I would get a rash on my chest and this was so itchy. I used to think that it was some foliage in the jungle that I had been in contact with.

It was a long time before I learned the truth. Five years after the end of the war, I went to Roehampton Hospital for a tropical disease check-up and from my blood tests, it was discovered that I had Helminthiasis (strongyloides with a creeping eruption).

When living and working in the marshy jungle with bare feet, small worms entered the cuts in my skin and from then on continued to live on my blood. The rash and itch occurred when these worms were breeding. I suffered this until, at the age of sixty, I learned that a cure had been discovered. I went to a hospital in Liverpool where I was told that my blood contained ten times the anti-bodies of a normal person. To be cured, I had to swallow several large detestable tablets. From then on, I was free of the horrible itch.

Every day I worked alongside men I did not know. Words were exchanged only when necessary. Thoughts were on other things: how or if we would survive and what was happening to our families back home. At the start of each working day, we omitted the formality of introductions - cursed our luck - worked in silence.

Mercifully, the rains eased off, but the workload did not and on we went, hacking down trees and levelling the earth. In dense jungle one's views are very limited and only when we had cleared a stretch of straight road did we observe that there were hills to climb, so as the road started to go upward, it needed to zig zag.

At times the turns were so acute that we doubted whether any vehicles would manage to negotiate them, but on we worked and after many days found ourselves digging out a shelf on a steep slope. Then, a strange thing happened. We heard voices. We were stunned into silence. How could anyone be there?

It was uncanny. We all stood stock-still and listened. Voices were there sure enough, and all the while we worked and wondered - who were they and where were they – and could they hear us?

We later learned that we'd been working at the head of a gorge and the voices were from the party working from the Burma side. They'd been on the other side of the valley but we could not see each other for trees.

I was curious to learn what was on the other side and sometime later I did, but it was an extremely painful experience. It was when the road was finished and the Japanese wanted to move some stores. They evidently could not produce a single truck to move these urgently needed goods and of course we were at hand.

About twenty of us were detailed to follow a guard into a hut on the floor of which was an assortment of sacks and boxes. As we entered we were allocated one of these. George Kershaw and I were extremely unlucky to be given one of the sacks. I was unable to lift mine from the ground, so one Jap and a POW raised it and settled it on my back. I shrank, not because of just the weight, but through pain.

The sacks contained iron hooks with very sharp points. These points stuck into my flesh and I could do nothing to ease the pain. I just staggered along behind the others. We climbed the zig zag and on up the valley. I don't know how I kept going. My legs wobbled and I reeled from side to side.

Once or twice I nearly went over the edge. I was thankful when the guard shouted: "Yasume" and, as I collapsed onto my knees, two POWs ran to lift the load from my back.

When the Jap saw the cuts on my back, he gave me a different sack. We continued on past the place where we had heard the voices and, reaching the top of the hill, gained a panoramic view of - ? BURMA.

Road Repairs

One or two Jap trucks started to use the road, but the rains made it almost impassable. They became bogged down every few hundred yards and had to be manhandled by us. We had to almost lift those mud-covered vehicles and we ended up covered in mud from head to foot so that we could hardly recognise each other.

Several times out hearts sank when we were called out in the middle of the night. We would have to run along the track in the dark to a spot where a truck was in difficulty. Bad tempered guards shouted and bullied, and it often took an hour or so to get it moving. Weary and absolutely worn out, we would wander back to camp and have a little sleep before reveille and more work.

So the road had to be improved. The sergeant (GUNSO) took charge. His first idea was to use what was already available: timber - we were surrounded by it. Thus it was that we became tree fellers. Our daily task was to fell twenty trees of a certain size, dress off the side branches and deliver them to the gunso on the road.

This often meant felling thirty trees. We were taught a lesson about forest vegetation. The creepers and the vines were so strong that they bound together the tops of the trees. It amazed us to discover that, having chopped through the trunk, the tree would refuse to fall. We would often have to push the severed trunk off its base and it would just fall to the ground and remain standing upright.

Often one would be left swinging to and fro, the top held tightly by the overhead vines. On the track the gunso had the bright idea to lay these timbers in rows of three. These rows were a wheel width apart and he seemed pleased with his efforts, that is until the first truck came along. Its front wheels pressed down the front of the log and the back end of the same log came up and jammed above the back wheels.

Evidently the logs had to be fastened in some way. Within a few days the Japs produced iron dogs. These had sharp points which were hammered into adjacent logs: this really annoyed us. The Japs used to say that they could not get food transported to us, yet they'd had no trouble getting these dogs.

We were caught between two fires. We were delighted when the trucks became stuck and their ideas did not work, but dismayed when it created more work for us. All the effort put into the making of this road did not seem to be helping their war effort – and we were glad about that.

Footprints in the Sand

Some bad stretches of road were near to streams or wadis where hard core was available. Our task then was to fill baskets with rocks and carry them to the road where a guard pointed to where he wanted the load to be tipped. This was still hard work, but a change from tree felling. At least one was able to get out of sight from the guards for a while. Of course they bullied if the baskets were not really full, and shouted if you were too long bringing the load.

As we cleared all the rocks from nearby, so we were forced to look further afield and venture up and down stream. It was then that I chanced upon a delightful spot: a small glen where the waters divided and joined up again some twenty yards down. Between the two arms of the stream was a beautiful stretch of silvery sand.

In the midst of the dense jungle it was an idyllic little haven. I could not resist the temptation. I walked across the miniature beach and enjoyed the luxury of the feeling of the soft sand beneath my feet. I filled my basket and hurried back to the others in my group. I could not keep my find to myself and some of the others followed me on the next trip. I let them go ahead of me and from the cries of delight, I knew they felt as I did. But their shouts suddenly died and they began to whisper and look around. They pointed to the sand where, to my surprise, were not only my prints but also those of a large cat.

From the spoors it was evident that the creature had come to drink. How close might it still be? How close was it when I made my last visit? The guard who was never far away and came to hurry us on and when we showed him the spoors, he gripped his rifle and peered into the undergrowth. He looked really scared and called to his friends.

We had three very scared guards gripping their rifles – and the word they spoke was - "TIGER".

From then on, I did not wander too far on my own.

Bullock Carts and Horse Flies

For several weeks we had seen about half-a-dozen oxen pulling carts up and down the road. Sometimes they would stop at our camps. We would load them up and off they would go. The poor beasts always looked so exhausted and we wondered if they were ever fed as there was no suitable pasture anywhere in the jungle.

We were not surprised then when, one by one, they died off and we were delegated to retrieve the cumbersome carts. The unfortunate beasts were left where they fell and they soon became the food larders of the area. When larger predators weren't feeding on them, thousands of ants and flies swarmed all over them.

As we passed we could hear the buzzing as they reduced the carcasses. On flight these insects were so numerous as to appear as a cloud. Little did we realise what effect the loss of these oxen would have on us. We paraded one morning to find ourselves facing a line of carts. We had the usual Tenko and then: "Ichi ni san men, ichi ni san men." Each three men were directed towards a cart. I was in the last group. A second Jap appeared at the door of a hut and signalled us inside.

There were stacks of what looked like ammunition boxes. We were to carry these out to the carts and when at last the guards were satisfied about the load, we were ordered to proceed. The carts alone were heavy but loaded up were almost impossible to shift. We failed to move them and the guards went into their usual tantrums. They kicked at the wheels and pushed from the back, but those vehicles stayed lodged in the soft earth.

"More men." Two extra men were assigned to each cart. We arranged to have two in the shafts and three pushing and were able to move very slowly forward. The track was far from level and sometimes we were heaving and sweating up steep banks and sometimes careering downward, dangerously near to disaster. We were all barefooted, and usually at the bottom of these runs were dried up streams and so we had great difficulty controlling the cart and trying to protect our feet from the jagged rocks. On level stretches the going was easier and we were able to regain our breath.

And More Horse Flies

"How far? Kilometres?" someone enquired of the guard. "Ju ni, ju ni," was the reply.

"Eight bloody miles!" "Meshy?" enquired another making the usual mime of shovelling rice into his mouth. "Campo," was the reply.

So we had to manhandle these carts eight more miles before we could eat and already we were feeling the pangs of hunger. One pint of breakfast rice soon became a memory.

And so for several days, this was our task, pulling loaded carts from one camp to the next. Of course there were obstacles of a different kind to overcome. The thousands of horse flies swarming near the carcasses were also partial to human blood and they must have been able to smell us. They were lying in wait for us. There were howls from our teams as these ravenous insects bit deep and sucked their fill. Their bites were like plungers penetrating the skin, and as men used their hands to ward them off, the carts would go out of control.

We became familiar with these places en route and would set up speed when nearing them, each time running the gauntlet, screaming like banshees and howling with pain when being attacked by these dreaded flies.

Sometimes we suspected that the boxes on the carts were ammunition, but it was useless to complain. On one trip, however, we carried some small wooden kegs of the type we'd often seen around the Jap cookhouse, and when out of sight of the guards I prized one open to reveal some brown paste. I took a finger full and tasted it: it was insipid, no horrid, but it might be some flavouring the Japs used in cooking so I swallowed a mouthful before replacing the lid.

We arrived at 10km camp and the last vehicle to pull in was squeaking rather loudly. The Jap in charge promptly came to our cart, took out the keg I'd opened and proceeded to thicken all the axles with the paste I had just swallowed!

These journeys through the jungle were taxing enough for fit men but for sick and starving prisoners, they were too much, and as they dropped out and had to be taken back to camp, so our workforce dwindled until only two carts operated.

Many of those who dropped out were transferred to a hut across the river – a so called hospital. The next move from there was to the clearing designated as the graveyard. Each death created more work for the living.

I was determined to keep going, but for how long?

The Boar

One morning I was surprised to be beckoned by one of the guards and ordered to get on the back of a truck. There were a few tools on board and we travelled for some distance along the road before stopping. Along the track ahead were pools of water, and after miming the task he wanted me to do, he drove off.

I was to dig holes off the side of the road, then cut a narrow trench from the pool to the hole. Having cleared one pool, I'd walk up the road to the next and repeat the operation. At least I was on my own and no bullying guards around, so quite enjoyed the experience of being a solitary human in this wild and hostile environment.

As the distance to the camps both ways was about five miles and there were many miles of uninhabited land to the North and South, I mused that I may be the only human in a few hundred square miles of jungle.

There was the constant background noise of the forest creatures, and the occasional cry of an animal unknown. I was constantly looking around and always aware of my vulnerability. I found myself gripping my shovel every time there was a rustle in the foliage nearby.

On one occasion I turned in the direction of one such noise to behold a strange sight. A frog was leaping for all its worth, followed by a lizard whose legs were working ten to the dozen – followed by a snake. Another few seconds and it would have been the end for the frog and lizard, but as I had my shovel at the ready, I clouted the snake as it passed (not hard enough to kill it, but certainly to deprive it of its lunch).

By the time the sun was getting low, I'd drained around twenty pools and covered a couple of miles of road. I was beginning to get anxious. I hoped the Japs would not forget me and hoped that they would not leave it too late.

Then I picked up the sound of a vehicle so started to walk in that direction. As the truck came into view, so did something else. A large and horrid boar scared and running from the truck was heading straight towards me. It was squealing loudly.

On both sides of this stretch of road was a wall of debris, tree trunks and branches; everything that had been cut down in the clearing of the road making it difficult for me or the boar to escape.

The screaming animal kept coming at me. I decided to match scream for scream and ran at it with my shovel at the ready. The nearer I got the louder I screamed and when only a few yards away, I was relieved to see it come to a sudden halt then turn and burrow itself through the brushwood and into the jungle.

The Japs had enjoyed the spectacle. I was pleased to get back on the truck.

Workmates

There were four of us from our regiment when we started off from Nakom Pathon and despite the tough trek up into the jungle, Sergeant Jack Robinson, Bombardier John Sugden and I managed to stay with the main party.

Our fourth member, Pat Geldart who was one of the strongest men in our battery, seemed to be among the leaders. So I was with men that I knew until we started work on the road, but then we soon became separated.

I then found myself with a group of Londoners who I got on with very well; Ted Corket was a rather gravel-voiced cockney character; Gouchy was a tall good-natured lad who had very flat feet and Sergeant Sid was a lively lad who fancied himself as an entertainer. They worked with me, felling trees, lifting them to one side, filling in and levelling off.

Toiling from morn till night in the hot sun wasn't easy and no matter how we worked, the guards always found an excuse to bully and shout.

Sadly, one by one these workmates fell sick and I was never to discover if they ever survived. I was a loner again joining any group assigned to me by the Japs. For a while, I worked with an Australian who said he was an all-in-wrestler and from his build, I could quite believe it. He died quicker than most. He stole some pork from the Jap cookhouse not knowing that the Japs had condemned it as unfit for consumption. So, I was a loner again.

Going out to work one morning from the camp at Tagaree, I could not but help overhearing a conversation and noted that the accents were from the North-East. Two men, one tall and one small, were discussing dance bands. Eventually, the taller of the two turned to me and said, "You are from our part of the world. Have you ever heard of this band?" I regretted that I had not.

He who had posed the question was George Kershaw and his friend was Stan Henson. I learned that Stan was a pianist and from then we often had music as a topic of conversation. Unfortunately, he too fell sick and was evacuated.

George was a survivor; in fact he was in every camp with me. I remember coming back to the hut in Tagaree to find him tending his fire on which a large container was boiling. When I asked him: "What's cooking?" he triumphantly said: "Snake!"

Life on the road was hell and it could be made worse by a bad tempered guard. Some were worse than others. One day the worst of them selected ten of us and marched us down the road. On reaching the work site he asked who was Gunso (Sergeant). When no-one answered up to being Sergeant, he evidently wanted the next in rank. As a bombardier, I suppose I was the senior so I stepped forward.

"You captain – you – all men work."

With that he stamped off and we started work. One lad in the group had dysentery and was forever popping off into the trees. At times he was away so long that I became anxious. During one of these anxious periods, the Jap arrived. He counted only nine men.

"Ku? - Ichi man? – Ichi man?" He went into a rage: "Ichi man!"

"Dysentery – taxan benjo," I tried to explain and pointed to where I thought the missing man was. The Jap would not be put off. He signalled me to go in the direction I had indicated and he followed. The sick man was nowhere to be seen and even though I shouted with all my might, there was no response. The Jap went berserk. He raved and shouted and then started to lay into me with his stick. In reeling to dodge the blows, I tripped backwards and whilst on the ground, he kicked me several times.

"Ichi! – Ichi!" he yelled and left.

It was evident that I had to find the man before he returned. We tried shouting together without result. We knew how easy it was to lose oneself in the forest and we were worried in case he had done just that. I decided to go further into the forest, but keep in touch with each other, so I posted one man on the road, a second within calling distance and a third further into the forest but within calling distance of the second. In that way we advanced calling out the whole time.

I was always ahead and became aware that I was walking on soft earth, then wet mud. Suddenly, the trees ended and there before me was a huge clearing. The whole area was soft earth and every inch was pitted with footprints. Thousands of animals of all kinds must have crossed this patch and many quite recently. It was an amazing sight. I was thrilled to just stand there.

A shout of: "Found him!" meant I had to return to the road. The Jap was there. He himself had found the sick man wandering aimlessly down the road. He realised the fellow was really ill.

I sat down to remove the leeches from my legs and feet and thought: "What did these b------ things feed on before we came here?"

Yorky

I never ever found out his name, nor did I ever discover how he came to be lost in the jungle, but I do know that Yorky was extremely lucky to escape a lonely and horrible death. Just over five feet tall, but quite stockily built, he was easily identified when he spoke. He had a rich Yorkshire accent and a prominent jaw which always seemed to be at an angle. He was a good workmate and quite popular.

I've described how difficult life could be pulling bullock carts, and heavy rain made the task even more arduous. Not only did the wheels sink in the mud, but also our bare feet slipped on the wet surface. Trying to pull up slopes found us on our knees, tugging the rope with one hand and digging toes and fingers into the earth and gaining a few feet after a shout of, "Heave!"

It was this that saved Yorky's life.

Because of heavy rainfall we'd made very slow progress that trip, so slow that the sun was down and we were still a couple of miles from camp. On a slope we'd just finished, a shout of "Heave!" when we heard a faint cry coming from the jungle.

"Listen everyone," said a sergeant, and the cry came again. It was eerie. Who or what could be out there? The Japs mumbled something to each other and gave permission to investigate. Guided by the calls, they found Yorky, and what a sorry state he was in. He was covered in leeches. They were in every crevice of his face and body.

The Japs lit cigarettes and burned them, while our fellows spat on their thumbs and stroked them off. They stood him up and got him back to the carts. Of course we had all managed to collect a few of these loathsome bloodsuckers for ourselves.

And so it was a very tired and weary work party that arrived back in camp that night plus of course one very lucky Yorkshireman. He'd got himself lost and worn himself out trying to find the camp. His biggest mistake was lying down in a jungle reputed to be one of the most leech infested in the world. However, what else could he have done in the circumstances, I just don't know.

Down by the River

It had become a ritual to make for the nearest water after work was finished. I suppose it was a way of washing away the dirt and the cares of the day's toll and to clean the clothes we'd been wearing. It was usual to jump straight in and then remove the clothing. After squeezing, thumping and pummelling, the garments were laid out to dry whilst we went back to bathe. As time went by, so did our clothes, and as the Japs did not supply any replacements, except the occasional jap happy, then there was very little laundering to be done

During our first few days at Tagaree, there were dozens bathing after work was finished, but as numbers decreased, we had the river to ourselves. There came a time when I was the sole bather, and one time I will never forget.

In the dry season there was never much water in the river so, after washing my jap happy and putting it to dry, I wandered downstream to find a pool in which I could immerse myself. I found one and really enjoyed the luxury of the cool water. Suddenly, above the noise of the forest, I heard voices: children's voices? They could not be – I had not even caught sight of any children for months. How would children get up here to this part of the country? I must be mistaken.

No, there they were again. I went back upstream and was amazed to see three native women and several children washing near where I'd left my one and only piece of clothing.

I do not know who would be most surprised. What would they think on seeing a naked white man with a red beard walking up the middle of the river towards them? The young ones went quiet. The women went on with the washing. What to do? I must get my jap happy.

I sat down in a shallow pool with my back to them pretending to wash my feet. I then turned onto my front hoping that I might be able to swim, but only scraped my chest. In the end I just had to be brave. I walked right past them, retrieved that which I'd left, and hurried out of sight.

The Jap Officer

One morning I was boiling water for the hospital patients when the Jap corporal came over. He ordered me to follow him and we went across the road. We were heading for the Jap camp and this was the first time I had been on that side. He led me past one or two huts and onto a smaller hut quite separate from the others.

"Nippon Officer – BIYOKI," said the corporal pointing inside, and there in a single bed lay the said gentleman. Up until then I had not been aware that there was an officer in the camp. We'd never seen him around.

I was led to the Jap cookhouse and given two bowls: one with some sort of liquid and the other with what looked like pieces of fruit. "Officer," said the corporal pointing towards the small hut. I entered the hut, coughed once or twice, and finally had to give the man a nudge. He opened his eyes: "Malaria – malaria," he murmured and closed his eyes again. I tried again but he only shook his head.

I must have stood there for quite some time wondering if he wanted the food, and also wondering what it tasted like. At last I made up my mind to try it. I went round the back of the hut, settled against a tree and ate the lot. What a disappointment. Nothing like bacon and eggs!

The pieces of fruit were sickly sweet, but what a change from our rice and gippo. I even licked the bowls clean before washing them in the river. Next morning I looked in at the sleeping commandant and then reported to the cookhouse. Again, I was given the two bowls, and again the Officer showed no interest.

I thought of Pat Geldart in the hospital hut across the river and wondered if he would like to taste the Officer's fare. It was not far to the river and I waded over, found Pat and we sat on the edge of his slats and finished a Japanese breakfast.

On the third morning I collected the bowls and noticed that there were some pieces different from previous days. I could not resist sampling these and the contents of the bowls were somewhat depleted by the time I reached his hut. To my horror, the Officer was sitting upright and looked much better. Fearing the worst, I handed him the bowls. He just looked at them and nodded. That was a signal to withdraw and I was glad to be off.

To this day I don't know if I was supposed to sit outside his place and await his beck and call. Luckily for me he must have slept right through his fever.

Camps

Of necessity the camps were sited near to rivers or streams and to the best of my knowledge were called, Eakin, Minoa, Tagaree and Border camp. These names were gleaned from the guards and whether the words meant anything or not I don't know.

From entries in my Pitman's Pocket Dictionary I know I was in Minoa on 14

April, and Tagaree on the 15th. On the 16th I arrived at Border camp and stayed there for just over five weeks. On 25 May, I returned to Tagaree.

The huts in all these camps were, to say the least, primitive. Some were worse than others. Some huts did not even have walls and so had no headroom. One had to crawl in and out.

In Tagaree however the main hut was fairly large and high and it was here I spent about twelve weeks. More than two hundred men were crowded into this with the Doctor at one end. A huge colony of gibbons inhabited that area and every morning we were awakened by them.

Not only did they create a din with their high-pitched "Whoop, whoop, whooping" but also they would often crash through foliage and sometimes drop onto our hut and scramble along the roof. It seemed that dawn was party time for them. Night time was very quiet in and around the hut. There were no lights and fires were a luxury and a necessity. Some men were content to just lie on their slats with their own private thoughts. A few sat round the fire staring into the flames rarely making conversation. Laughter was now a rarity. Occasional moans came from the sick.

I still found comfort in my guitar, but now played quietly to myself. The sad men sitting around me were in no mood for singsongs. However, some of them must have listened and appreciated, for often a chap would come to me and say which was the last tune I'd been playing before he fell asleep.

Very few were smoking. There was very little tobacco to be had, and my heart went out to those men who craved a smoke and were reduced to begging the odd draw from anyone with a cigarette. Mind you, to call them cigarettes was a gross exaggeration. Anything wrapped in any old scrap of paper helped to satisfy the craving.

I'm glad I did not smoke.

A Day to Remember

For several days everything was very quiet. Only two or three of us were doing odd jobs around the camp. Boiling water for the sick was a priority. There was a marked absence of Japs. No work of any kind was being done on the road.

There were less than forty in our hut, which was once full and nearly all of them were ill. Although still on my feet, I was not feeling very good and I was doing simple tasks at half my normal speed and feared that I may be going down with a fever.

On the morning of 18 August, I had reason to go to the bog, and as I was making water, I happened to look down, and to my horror noted that what was coming from me was black. Even in the hot sun, I shivered: "Was this really coming from me?" I could not believe it.

"What on earth have I got?"

I felt desperate. Instead of going back to the hut I walked into the jungle. "Was this the end? Was this going to finish me off when I fought so hard and kept going until now?"

I thought of all the men I'd seen laid in holes in the ground in this foreign land and dreaded that it should happen to me.

"I must keep going. I must get back home. What would my family do?" My thoughts were in turmoil and suddenly I found myself on the edge of the road. Thank goodness something happened to take my mind off the problem.

Across the Jap compound there was smoke: "Why do they have a fire this early?" I crept quietly through the trees and was surprised to see nearly all the guards squatting round a fire, and their conduct was suspicious.

They were speaking in low tones (unusual for Japs) and were sorting through bundles of papers. Sometimes they would pass a sheet of paper round and after a nod from all of them it would be put onto the flames.

This procedure went on for as long as I observed them. Their mood; the serious look on their faces; the urgency they displayed in selecting these papers for burning convinced me that there was something serious afoot.

We POWs knew that the Japs were under orders not to leave any prisoners behind if they had to retreat. We were to be disposed of.

I hurried back to the hut to appraise the doctor and the others of what I'd witnessed. And so it happened that about a dozen of us were standing at the entrance of our hut when the corporal came over.

He was the only Jap with a smattering of English.

He was very quiet and looked perturbed. He then spoke words which were to be the most welcome we'd heard for many a year.

"War finish – England – Japan - shake hands. All men go home." "OK," he added and then turned and walked slowly off.

We were dumbstruck. For a while we just stared at each other.

"Is it true?" we asked each other. WE LAUGHED - WE CRIED.

CHAPTER 12

Going Home????

"War finished. All men go home." We had waited three-and-a-half years to hear these words.

My thoughts flashed from one thing to another: home, family, dad, mother, sisters, friends.

The Jap corporal reappeared with several guards carrying rifles: "All men go!"

Evidently, we were to move immediately and to the coast. I collected my guitar and a few treasures but instead of staying with the main party, I slipped through the trees and waded the river to see Pat. He was from my battery and his army number was next to mine. Yes, he was 919804 and mine was 919805. What a coincidence that we should be the only two from our regiment left in this part of the world.

But what of Jack and John also from my battery? Were they still on the road? Were they still sick? Had they heard that the war was finished? I reached Pat: he was in a terrible fever. He was so delirious that he could not appreciate the joy of the moment. When at last I got him to his feet, he pointed to the chap who had been his companion in distress: "Wake him – tell him!" I realised that this was impossible. Tragically, the poor fellow was dead and was never to savour the sweet taste of freedom.

I said a quiet prayer.

"Come on Pat. WE ARE GOING HOME!"

We staggered out on the road and joined a string of stragglers. What should have been a joyful parade was a really sad sight. Sick men walked like zombies, but with a determined set look on their faces. Every step was an effort. Some wandered from side to side. Along came two guards and started to bully the weary stragglers pushing them with their rifle butts. Once or twice I had to get behind Pat to prevent him from such treatment.

A terrible thought came to me. What if the Japs were lying? What if the war was not finished? We dared not stop lest we could not get to our feet again. At long last we reached Minoa, and after being given the usual rice and gippo, we just settled down anywhere we could and slept.

Going Home

On the next morning we assembled to find our numbers were further depleted. Several, including Pat, had been kept behind as needing special further treatment. We who were left trudged on and finally practically collapsed into the next camp.

Some medical orderlies met us to assist the stragglers and one of them was most interested in my guitar: "Can you play?" he asked. He was a Eurasian lad, probably a Singapore volunteer.

"We have had no music at all. Would you play round the huts?" When I replied in the affirmative, he was delighted and whilst still helping one poor straggler, he led me down into the camp.

What I saw appalled me. I'd seen some bad camps in my years as a POW, but this was the worst ever. Not surprising it was called "Death Valley".

The first hut I approached had no walls. I had to sit at the entrance and peer in. The smell was terrible and not one of the inmates could even stir. The glad news of the end of the war had not done much to revive these poor devils. After a few songs I moved to the next hut. It was of similar construction to the last and once again I sat at the entrance and started to play.

Imagine my absolute surprise when two of the inmates immediately sat up: John Sugden and Jack Robinson! They were safe, but far from well. They'd both had a rough time, and after exchanging a few words, I continued my round.

Another great surprise was in store for me. I found Stan Henson, the piano player from South Shields. I finished off at a hut where the chaps there had not been able to cope with the strain. They seemed drained and unable to appreciate what was going on around them.

After another rice and gippo meal, I just collapsed into the nearest empty space and slept. The following day we made better progress. From time to time a lorry passed us and we presumed that it was transporting the very sick and lame. To our delight we finally got a view of the sea and realised that we were nearing the end of our trek.

Kirrikan

The huts at this camp by the sea were an improvement on any camp up country, but the food was only slightly better. However, we realised that we were nearer to civilisation and food could be obtained at the village. That is if one had any money (I only now realised that for the past few months I'd never even seen money much less held any). Should we not have been paid for working on the road, even the paltry 10 cents a day? Were the Japs pocketing it?

After being in an enclosed atmosphere in the jungle, it was most refreshing to sit on the beach and look at the sea, and after a few days I could discern an island.

Help began to reach us from Nakom Pathon and among the relief party was Paddy Cusack who had been a close friend and singing partner at that camp.

Planes began to drop supplies. The first article we received was a mosquito net. We'd had no mossie nets since our stay in India. It was a prime example of "closing the stable door". We'd rather have had a packet of biscuits or a bar of chocolate - but they did come in useful: we went up to the village and flogged them for just over thirty bahts.

I'd not seen an egg for months so purchased a basket of eggs and a jar of pork fat. How I enjoyed sitting at my little fire making one omelette after another. I made one large special and took it to John and Jack.

On 31 August an officer entered the camp: he was quite an imposing figure, over six feet tall and wearing a uniform quite strange to us. The Yanks in our hut boasted that he was a GI, whilst the Aussies declared that he was one of theirs.

However, when he shouted: "Gather round chaps," we knew that he was ours. We were eating our meal of rice and gippo and took it with us. The Officer took a look into my Dixie and was disgusted: "What on earth is that?" We explained that what we were eating was an immense improvement on what we'd had for the last few years.

Then occurred something that convinced us that we'd really won the war. The Officer waved the senior Jap to his side and practically threw the contents of the Dixie at him: "This food is not good enough. Get them something better."

For the first time we saw a Japanese Officer cringe. Our Officer then gave us a short talk and explained that he was giving each of us a small piece of paper on which we must write our home address on one side and a brief message on the other. He assured us that he would make it a priority for these messages to reach our loved ones.

I wrote: "SAFE – HOME SOON – LOVE LEN."

I still have this piece of paper because my mother kept it among her treasures until she died at the age of 94.

With Jack and John under hospital care and Pat left behind at the last camp, I was a loner again and found myself in a small hut with Yanks and Aussies. I may have been the only British present.

In POW life we had to suffer much criticism from the colonials; they blamed us for their predicament; they blamed Churchill – Wavell – Percival; everyone and everything British. After the arrival of the English Officer, their attitude changed somewhat.

They did not know I was listening, but after dark that night I had a quiet smile to myself. The Yanks were very impressed by his efficiency; the Aussies admired his uniform and bearing. From then the conversation turned to British inventions and achievements. I did not realise that we were so good and fell asleep feeling smug and contented.

Meanwhile, there were still Japs in the camp and some were still doing guard duty. One armed sentry was patrolling a sandbag emplacement. When he was off into the trees to have a smoke, a couple of Aussies and I nosed round and found some steps leading to an underground room.

From the light coming down the stairway, we perceived shelves full of Thai silk. One Aussie declared that he was going to be married as soon as he got home and his bride would look lovely in "That" and he grabbed "That" and made off. I grabbed the first and handiest roll and with the other Aussie went up to the village where we had no difficulty in exchanging silk for bahts.

I was now rich enough to buy as much food as I wanted. The rest of the money I stuffed into my guitar. After all, when one wears only a jap happy, where else can one keep one's cash!

Supplies were still being dropped, and no doubt the doctors would now have the medical equipment and medicines which they had not seen for years. Sadly, however, they were too late for one or two: they died and would never know the pleasure of freedom and the joyous reunion with loved ones at home.

What a tragedy! So near and yet so far! They'd only known the bitterness of defeat and were never to taste the sweetness of success. I went down to the solitude of the beach, gazed at the ocean and shed a quiet tear.

The Dakota

Rumours spread that we were going to be flown out and taken to Rangoon. The flat ground on which the supplies had been dropped needed to be extended and so we went to work again, clearing small trees and brush. This time we were not working for the Japs, so we worked with a will.

On 5 September a Dakota landed and we were ready and waiting. I think the Captain of the craft was a little apprehensive about the room for take-off and he requested us to travel as light as possible. So, as I walked towards the aircraft, I did something which later I was to deeply regret: I handed my guitar, with the money inside, to a young Thai lad who was with a group of interested bystanders.

This was my first plane flight and I spent quite a long time in the cockpit. All the crew were kind enough to sign their names in my Pitman's pocket book.

Flying Officer Robert D Lister wrote: "Certified flying at 7,000 feet." R. Sinclair, a navigator from Winnipeg, wrote: "14 degrees North, 97 degrees and 30 minutes east." They were a great crew.

Of course the lads who smoked managed to scrounge cigarettes from the airmen, their first "tailor-made" as they called them for many years. Our lads reciprocated by giving them some of their native shag. The crew coughed and spluttered and could not believe that anyone could smoke that and live!

We hit a few air pockets which alarmed us a little but managed to land safely at Rangoon airfield. After alighting we walked towards the nearest building and the first notice that caught my eye read: "Bring your foreign currency here and we will honour it." I had given all mine away!

We were led to a dining room: tables; chairs; tablecloths; knives; forks; spoons, and LADIES!

Lady Mountbatten had come out with the WVS.

It all seemed so strange. Sitting on a chair was odd. Picking up a knife and fork was a novelty. We looked at the food we had dreamed about and longed for, but were too filled with emotion to really appreciate.

The WVS ladies looked on sympathetically; we were having a weep.

Rangoon

After that first delicious meal, I was taken to St. John's Convent where two delightful nursing sisters met me: one hailed from Northern Ireland and the other came from Berwick.

Following a civilised bath, I was given a pair of pyjamas and a pair of slippers – AND A BED – to sleep in, with – SHEETS and PILLOWS. It all seemed so strange and I had almost to pinch myself to make sure that it was really happening.

I lay awake for quite some time that night, enjoying my newfound luxury and wondering what had happened to the other lads of my regiment. Had they survived? Where were they now? Were they also enjoying such luxury?

Next day I spent some time at the windows looking out onto a Rangoon street. What a change from being surrounded by forest! It was a novelty to see traffic. Several soldiers were in evidence and I ventured down to the front door to discover that they were the DLI. It was good to chat to them for most of them were familiar with my hometown.

From them I also learned that many of my regiment were a few miles away at 5 FAHRU. Without hesitation I walked up the road in the direction they had pointed. I was wearing my pyjamas and slippers, but after years in a jap happy, I felt dressed.

Not only did I find 5 FAHRU, but also found Conlin, Glancy and several more of the regiment. "Our Come and Join Us Troup" were reunited. They were overjoyed to see me too, especially as they had heard rumours that I had died. I stayed with them for two days before setting off very early on a misty morning to try and find my way back to the convent.

Those two delightful sisters really scolded me and before I knew it they had jabbed my arms with several needles before confining me to barracks.

On 10 September, Air Marshall Sir Keith Parkes visited us and gave a talk. There was a loud cheer when he announced that a dozen ships had arrived and within ten days twelve thousand of us would be on our way home.

He also assured us that we would have excellent care on the way to Blighty and we would be fitter and stronger by the end of the voyage. That day I was discharged from hospital, given green tropical kit and told, to my delight, that I was being sent to 5 FAHRU.

I would be with my pals again.

Back with the Family

To say that I was happy to arrive at 5 FAHRU and be with my friends is an understatement. We'd lived in each other's company for more than six years, so we were more like family. We'd been through thick and thin.

We'd joined the Territorial Army in the spring of 1939; were called up together; lived in tents; slept on floors in castles and old houses; on Norfolk beaches; in freezing cold Nissen huts in Scotland; in ship's holds in trenches and dug-outs and in POW camps.

Now we were reunited, and everyone had a tale to tell. We also had visits from members of the regiment who were at camps nearby. All were elated at the thought of going home together. It was like old times.

On the morning that we were due to sail, I went to the ablutions room to wash and shave. Right down the centre of the room was a long bench with a basin and tap every few feet. At head height was a narrow board on which, above every tap, was a piece of polished tin, which served as a mirror.

As I scraped away my whiskers, a chap opposite looked through and said: "Hi Len, how's Monsoon?" He was referring to a descriptive piece of music I'd written for the orchestra at Nakom Pathon.

Immediately, a fellow a few feet away, said: "Monsoon. Who wrote Monsoon?" When I owned up he said: "We are broadcasting from Rangoon station tonight, and we are playing your piece." Of course, I embarked on the MV *Empire Pride* a few hours later and so never had the opportunity of hearing it!

"C'est la vie."

Crossing the Bay of Bengal was really rough. We were tossed about so much that men could not eat the food they had looked forward to for so many years. I was not affected and found myself collecting rations for a full table of 14 and often there was only myself to eat.

Colombo

If our arrival in Colombo was a relief, it was also spectacular. Bands were playing on the quayside; flags were flying; sailors on craft moored in the harbour cheering and people waving. What a welcome!

We were met by WRENS AND WAAF's who played "nursemaid" to us. They opened doors, helped us onto trucks and guided us to a rendezvous with the Red Cross where we were given lunch.

Later, whilst the others were having a post lunch break, I wandered out onto the street and eventually found myself at the entrance to a large open building. There seemed to be some sort of Bazaar going on. A few native lady customers were outnumbered by the young nuns who were in attendance. One of the latter motioned to me to enter and a second offered me a cool drink. A third showed me a stool and soon I became the centre of interest. Everyone of them seemed anxious to talk and to be of some service.

As I was not a Catholic, I had never previously conversed with nuns, but these sisters of the church were so relaxed and spoke delightful English. They coyly asked questions about England, my home and my family, and we discussed the sadness of war and hopes for the future.

These sisters were so calm and so sincere and so peaceful. There was an aura of serenity – a perfect antithesis to the horrors of life in Japanese POW camps.

I felt at peace with the world as I made my way back to the harbour.

Our departure from Ceylon was even more memorable than our arrival. Bands played us off from the quayside, crowds waved and cheered and every ship in the harbour hooted the victory V signal. The noise was deafening – it was exhilarating. It made us proud to be part of the great British family of nations.

Half-Way Home

From Colombo we had a smoother passage across the Indian Ocean and into the Red Sea. At Adablya we went ashore to be kitted out for cold climate.

I found the Suez Canal most interesting but was very disappointed in the Mediterranean Sea. Far from being the blue I expected, it was very dull and grey. We had sunless skies and misty rain for most of the way.

We started to feel the cold after Gibralter and when we finally reached Liverpool, we had to lie off because of fog (I think that was the reason but there may have been a dispute with the Dockers).

When we finally docked we noticed dozens of cars lining the quayside. The warm-hearted car owners of the city of Liverpool had volunteered to chauffer us to our destination which was the Transit Camp at Poverty Lane.

Crowds lined the streets and cars drove very slowly. People, especially women and children, shook our hands through open windows.

One lady put her head into our window and then in a loud voice proclaimed to the world: "Eeh, they're only bairns!"

That hurt me a little. I thought of all that I had been through in the last six years and reckoned that was enough for a lifetime.

On the other hand, I should have been pleased that in spite of all that the Japs had thrown at me, I'd not only survived but also still had my youthful appearance.

We were now only a few dozen miles from home and could not understand why we were not setting off immediately. We had to stay there a few days for medicals and documentation.

The final stage of our homecoming was exceedingly tedious. We were too anxious and the train seemed too slow. When at last we reached Newcastle, there was a Sunderland corporation bus waiting for us and we were taken speedily to the Town Hall in Fawcett Street, Sunderland.

No one could possibly describe the feelings we had when we first saw members of our families. It had been more than four years since we'd seen any of them. A tall attractive young lady ran at me and threw her arms around me. I was taken aback and as my father was shaking my hand, I looked over the young woman's shoulder and said: "Who is this?"

It was my second sister Jennie who had been a schoolgirl when I last saw her.

Home at Last!

The drive home was along a route I had walked a thousand times. We passed all the old familiar places, places I once doubted I would ever see again. We turned into our street bedecked with flags and welcome home banners. A crowd of well-wishers were crowded around the door and it was with difficulty we managed to get into the house.

And there stood my mother as I'd pictured her many times: tears in her eyes, lips quivering, speechless and ready to fling her arms around me.

At last I was introduced to a young lady. It couldn't be my baby sister? It was. Next day we went down to the station to meet Irene. She'd managed to get leave from the Land Army; our family was now complete.

That night was a family party. Grandmother arrived tearful. Aunt Gladys and Uncle Chris arrived next door with three daughters and once again, I had to face three young ladies I'd remembered as children. Uncle Fred remarked that I now talked "posh".

I had been sitting next to a debonair young man for some time when Uncle Jack asked me what I'd thought of the "Bold William". It then came to me that the debonair young man was none other than my little cousin Billy. How he'd grown!

Aunties arrived shedding tears. It was all very emotional, but I remained calm.

It wasn't until a day later that my mother asked Jennie to give me her surprise. She sat down at the piano and played quite beautifully The Warsaw Concerto.

It was then I let the tears flow. I was home with my loved ones.

My war was over.

That night I gazed at the ceiling from the comfort of my bed. I couldn't believe my luck. How had I survived? Why had I been spared?

Every day for more than three years I had seen men die: die because of Japanese inhumanity; starved of food and denied basic medicines that would have kept them alive. Men knew death was inevitable but faced it bravely and with dignity. They were never to know that the Germans and Japanese would be defeated. They were never to know the joy of freedom. They were never to know the sweetness of success but only the bitterness of defeat. Never to know if they'd given their lives in vain.

What a tragedy! What a waste!

CHAPTER 13

Life After the End of WWII

After only a few days at home, I was sent to Ryhope General Hospital. I opened my eyes one morning to see a lovely little nurse: it was Ruby. We married on 10 August 1946 and the wedding ceremony took place in the Minster which in those days was known as "Bishopwearmouth".

On Boxing Day 1947 our son David was born and in 1949, we were delighted to be blessed with a daughter we named Jennifer.

Ruby and I were to spend seventy happy years together.

David and Jennifer Gibson

I was determined not to go back to working in the factory, so I attended a course at Washington Civil Resettlement Unit, then another at Welbeck Abbey followed by some time spent at Chester Road Senior Boys' School observing. I subsequently went to Moot Hall in Newcastle to be interviewed and was given a place in an Emergency College.

My first position was in Thomas Street Primary School and my second was at Commercial Road Juniors where I spent seventeen happy years. I was then promoted to Deputy Head of Hasting Hill School where I spent another enjoyable seventeen years: I taught general subjects but became well known as a music teacher because of my guitar. To give members of staff a free period, I would take the whole school for singing.

For the EDA I spent several years doing a Summer school course and had approximately thirty teachers in the classes which were held in colleges in Durham City, including six nuns, six headteachers and twenty others.

1969 Len Gibson Summer School at St Hild College, Durham City

Health

As previously described I had a lot of trouble with stomach pains, but one of the worst things I suffered with was the rash which caused violent itching.

I was sent to Roehampton Hospital in London where it was discovered that I had Helminthiasis. When working barefooted in the jungle, certain tiny worms had crept into the cuts in my feet and then worked their way through the whole of my body.

There was no known cure at that time, and I suffered with this condition until the age of sixty when I read of a cure. The cure came from Liverpool and I subsequently attended the Liverpool School of Tropical Medicine where I saw Professor Geoff Gill. He asked me if I could give them some of my blood for research purposes.

FEPOW Clubs

I became a member of the Fellowship of the Services and usually helped with the entertainment at each monthly meeting.

We FEPOWs formed a club called "The Changi"; I was the Treasurer and Welfare Officer. I visited the sick and needy in homes or hospitals using my bicycle as I had no car. I organised trips into the country for the children where everyone who ran a race won a prize.

South Shields FEPOW Club.

I later joined the South Shields FEPOW Club. As Secretary, I organised lunch meetings and holiday trips. I also ran a raffle each Christmas, usually raising £1,000. With this money, we took all the widows to a show at the *Empire* followed by a meal at a local café. I always took my guitar so that we could have a singsong. We loved to get together.

Celebrations

To celebrate the 60th anniversary of peace, there was a special lunch at the Sea Hotel in South Shields. I invited the Lord Lieutenant and his wife, Mayor of Sunderland and his wife, Mayor of South Shields and his wife, and the widows of those who held the Victoria Cross and Double George Cross. The ladies were given orchids to wear.

We had a toast to the Queen, followed by the FEPOW prayer and then enjoyed a happy singalong.

I have lovely letters of praise and thanks from all who attended.

There was a special service held in Durham Cathedral and I was invited to say a prayer. My wife and two sisters accompanied me. Imagine our surprise when a lady on duty at the door would not let us in as the church was full. Only when I explained who I was and that I was to say a prayer were we admitted.

What a marvellous view from the high pulpit. I'll never forget it!!

Dave Stewart

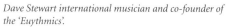

Dave Stewart international musician and co-founder of the 'Euythmics'.

Wendy House for granddaughter Clare.

At the bottom of my garden in Ettrick Grove, Sunderland, I would often light a fire and sit there strumming and singing like I did in the POW camps.

My son's two friends, John Stewart and David Stewart were regular visitors, and the younger lad took a keen interest in my guitar.

He became a professional and teamed up with Annie Lennox to form the "Eurythmics".

There was also a large dog kennel in the garden and this became the gang hut for their "Bulldog Club". In the other corner, I made a little "Wendy House" for my granddaughter Clare.

Heroic Patient

With my wife I attended a reunion in the Festival Hall. The place was full and I suddenly caught sight of (Colonel) Weary Dunlop. Ruby and I had to fight our way to get near him and what a surprise when we found he was talking to Bill Brown, the lad who had held me during that appendix operation.

On 24 September 1987, I met Weary Dunlop again; he was with Jack Chalker and Lawrence van der Post. They were kind enough to sign my copy of Weary Dunlop's diary. Weary wrote: "To Len Gibson, one of my heroic patients. With every good wish 24 September 1987. *Weary E E Dunlop*."

Commercial Road School

At Commercial Road School, I was in charge of sporting activities and every Friday, after lessons, my room would be filled with young lads who were eager to be chosen for the football team. As I called out a name, I would throw them a strip and watch the delight on their faces.

We played home matches on the field next to the school, but away matches proved a little more difficult. I would put some on the bus and fill up my car.

(Left) Football team at Commercial Road School. (Right) Recently received photo from Keith Adams in Australia when he was footballer of the year at Hasting Hill Primary School.

Len Gibson giving a speech at Sunderland War Memorial – Image credit: Sunderland Echo.

On V J Days, I would ask my fellow FEPOW friends to meet with me at the War Memorial on Burdon Road, Sunderland.

I would conduct a little service and lay a wreath: some family and friends would attend. My mother always attended; even at a good age she came in her wheelchair often wrapped in her own Union Jack!

When our numbers decreased, there came a time when we joined up with the service held in November. I spoke the FEPOW prayer and have done so ever since.

I am always delighted to see so many people. The Sunderland folk always turn up in their thousands.

Of the many reunions and outings we had, there is one we'll never forget.

It was an invitation with thousands of war veterans to Doxford Hall. All we knew was that it was in Northumberland. After some great fun and excitement, we arrived at the gate and a person met us and showed us where to park.

Doxford Hall estate, VJ Day celebrations 2006.

Doxford Hall estate, VJ Day celebrations 2006.

After admiring the imposing building, we wandered round the lovely grounds. We were invited into the Hall and to our surprise, brought by a helicopter from RAF Boulmer, we were treated to fish and chips. We were then entertained and learned that our host was Mr. Brian Burnie.

Thank you, Mr. Burnie, for a superb experience.

Brian Burnie on his 7,000 mile charity walk, 2019.

The Millennium Maze at Doxford Hall, formally opened by war veterans in 2000.

A Visit from Japan

In the year 2020, I had a visit from a remarkable young Japanese girl; she spoke fluent English and had read my book. We discussed what had happened in Thailand and she asked my permission to have my thoughts published in the 'Tokyo Times'.

Later, I received a newspaper with two of my photographs, together with a letter in which she stated that "meeting you was one of the most fantastic memories I have of the UK".

We both expressed our desire to have children learn of the evils of war and the pleasures of peace. Her name was Chiaki Sawada and she certainly gave me food for thought.

A Wonderful Life

Soon I must say farewell to this beautiful world. I have loved its music and children; loved the earth with its trees and flowers; loved the song of the blackbird and the laughter of children.

I have had a wonderful life thanks to my wife Ruby who gave me seventy years of happiness and the love of the children she bore.

I hate war and the misery and hardship it brings, and I pray that the people of this world will learn to live in peace.

from Len.

Every year at the Remembrance Service, I recite the FEPOW prayer:

And we that are left to grow old with the years.

Remembering the heartache, the pain and the tears.

Hoping and praying that never again,

Man will sink to such sorrow and shame.

The price that was paid we will always remember.

Every day, every month, not just in November

Len Gibson and wife Ruby.

Len with children Jennifer and David.

Hasting Hill Primary School 1980 (Len Gibson front row, 4th from left).

With grandsons Andrew, James and John. 1980.

Len and Ruby with their first great grandchild.

Len Gibson receives the British Empire Medal from the Lord Lieutenant of Tyne and Wear, Mrs Sue Winfield OBE.
Image credit: North News and Pictures.

Len Gibson with his British Empire Medal supported by his family.
Images credit: North News and Pictures.

100th Birthday with Cllr David Snowdon, and Mayoress, Cllr Dianne Snowdon, 2020

VJ Day 75 - 15th August 2020 at Daft as a Brush Cancer Patient Care, Newcastle.
Left to right:- Pearly Mark, Brian Burnie, Len and Teresa.

Len with daughter Jennifer VJ Day 75, 2020. *A very special birthday cake, January 2021.*

Len's 101st Birthday, January 2021, with standard-bearers Bob Bulmer, Len Howie, Bob Hardy.

The Big Day

On Wednesday 19 May 2021 there was an event fitting for a hero.

A spitfire flypast, the Red Devils parachuting in, musical performances, a Northumbrian piper, male voice choir and 120 pupils of Hasting Hill Academy, where Len was Deputy Head for 17 years.

A celebration of Len's extraordinary life has put the spotlight on the charity close to his heart – Daft as a Brush Cancer Patient Care - as it extends free transport for cancer patients nationwide.

A brand new Daft as a Brush ambulance has been named 'Len Guitar Gibson' in honour of Len. Messages of support flooded in from all over the world, including Dave Stewart, Kate Adie CBE (Former Chief News Correspondent for BBC), Australian footballer Keith Adams and a host of others who have all been encouraged by Len's indomitable spirit.

Len with his new ambulance, named 'Len 'Guitar' Gibson'
Image: North News Pictures.

Herrington Country Park: 120 singing schoolchildren walk from Hasting Hill Academy, led by a Rothbury Piper and Daft as a Brush Cancer Patient Care Volunteers, to greet Len. Image: Tony Iley.

Images: North News and Pictures.

A spectacular Spitfire fly-past in honour of Len.
Images: North News and Pictures.

Lance Corporal Lee Crudgington of The Red Devils Display Team 'drops in' to deliver Len's newly revised book; "A Wearside Lad in World War II".

Pearly King and Queens from London entertain Len and guests before the celebration cake is cut with Daft as a Brush charity founder, Brian Burnie.
Images: North News and Pictures.

Len and Brian next to 'Len Guitar Gibson' - The first ambulance to serve cancer patients nationwide.

School Visit

10th June 2021, Len meets children at Hasting Hill Academy in West Herrington, Sunderland, where on his return from the Japanese prisoner of war camp he became deputy head teacher.

Schoolchildren asking Len questions about his former years at the school and as a Japanese prisoner of war. Images: North News and Pictures.

Brian Burnie and Len Gibson sign the display wall created by schoolchildren and teachers from the events of 19th May 2021.
Images: North News and Pictures.

LETTERS HOME

Letters 1, 2, 3

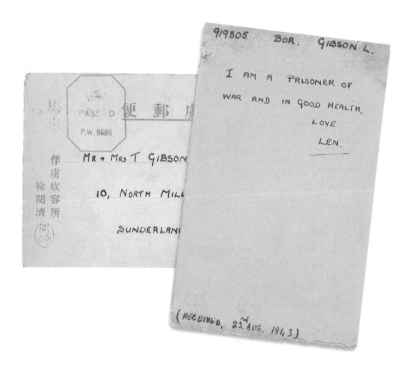

"I AM A PRISONER OF WAR AND IN GOOD HEALTH."
Received 23.08.1943

"SAFE. HOME SOON. LOVE LEN."
Sent 31.08.1945

"THAILAND."
Sent 04.09.1945

DEAR MOTHER

GOD HAS ANSWERED YOUR PRAYERS AT LAST. I AM EXPECTING AT ANY MOMENT A PLANE TO LAND ON THE FIELD, WHICH WILL BEAR US WITH GOOD SPEED PART OF THE JOURNEY, WHICH WILL BRING US BACK TO YOU ALL.

THIS LETTER IS INDEED HARD TO WRITE AS FOR THREE-AND-A-HALF YEARS WE HAVE HAD NO OPPORTUNITY TO WRITE AT ALL. BUT, NEVER MIND, I WILL LOOK FORWARD TO A REPLY AND I KNOW THAT YOU WILL WASTE NO TIME IN SENDING IT.

WE MAY SPEND A FEW WEEKS AT RANGOON FOR RECUPERATION PURPOSES, BUT THAT IS ALL FOR OUR OWN GOOD. HOW IS DAD? STILL GOING STRONG, I HOPE. HOW ABOUT A RIDE ON OUR BIKES, OR ARE YOU GOOD ENOUGH ON THE GUITAR TO GIVE ME A FEW LESSONS?

AND IRENE (MY LAP DOG), I THINK MYSELF MOTHER IS RIGHT AND I SHALL HARDLY RECOGNISE YOU. AND JENNIE (WITH PATHETIC BLUE EYES), I HOPE YOU HAVE HAD SUCCESS AT YOUR JOB AND ARE DOING THE WORK YOU LIKE.

AND WHAT ABOUT THE BABY OF THE FAMILY ENA. I BET YOU'RE A BIG BABY NOW AND PROBABLY WORKING TOO. YES, IT WILL BE GRAND TO SEE YOU AGAIN, AND GRAN, UNCLES, AUNTS AND COUSINS. I CAN'T WRITE TO THEM ALL BUT GIVE THEM MY REGARDS, AND I SHALL BE GLAD TO BE WITH YOU ALL AGAIN.

AS REGARDS ELSIE, I HAVE HAD ONLY ONE SMALL LETTER AND I WILL AWAIT A TELEGRAM INFORMING SITUATION. THAT IS ALL FOR NOW MOTHER, AND DON'T FORGET ALL OF YOU, KEEP YOUR CHINS UP AND WE'LL HAVE A GOOD CHRISTMAS THIS YEAR.

EVER YOUR LOVING SON.
LEN

Letter 5

Rangoon 06.09.1945

DEAR MOTHER

THE PLANE ARRIVED AND TOOK US ON A PLEASANT TRIP. I HAD A GOOD LOOK ROUND AND CHATTED ALL THE WAY TO THE CREW. THEY PUT US DOWN SAFELY, ALMOST WITHOUT A BUMP AT RANGOON AIRFIELD. FROM THERE WE WERE TAKEN BY AMBULANCE TO A RECEIVING STATION WHERE CERTAIN EXPERIENCES AWAITED US.

FIRSTLY, WE WERE GREETED BY EUROPEAN LADIES OF THE WVS (OUR FIRST SIGHT OF WHITE WOMEN FOR THREE YEARS). THEY WERE INDEED A PLEASANT SIGHT AND LOOKED AFTER US PRETTY WELL.

SECONDLY, WE SAT AT TABLES WITH WHITE COVERS AND FLOWERS IN THE CENTRE. WE HAD BREAD AND USED A KNIFE, FORK AND SPOON. THESE THINGS HAVE BEEN UNKNOWN TO US FOR YEARS. AND SO YOU SEE, WE ARE HAVING A GRAND TIME.

FROM THERE VERY NICE NURSES SAW US INTO TRUCKS AND WE WERE TAKEN TO A HOSPITAL. A SPRING BED WITH WHITE SHEETS WERE THE NEXT REVELATIONS: DIFFERENT TO A WEEK AGO SLEEPING IN THE WET JUNGLE WITH FIRES TO KEEP AWAY THE BEASTS AND LEECHES ATTACKING US ALL NIGHT LONG. AND SO HERE WE ARE LISTENING TO A RADIO AND I AM GOING TO SEE MY FIRST PICTURE SHOW.

TREATMENT IS EXCELLENT AND FOOD THE BEST. ALTHOUGH THEY ARE TREATING US AS PATIENTS, I AM IN EXCELLENT HEALTH HAVING RECOVERED FROM JUNGLE FEVERS SINCE WE RECEIVED NEWS OF PEACE ON 18TH OF LAST MONTH.

WE HAD TO TREK THROUGH THE JUNGLE 20 KILOMETRES TO THE COAST AND FROM THERE THE PLANES DID THEIR WORK, DROPPING FOOD BY PARACHUTE AS WELL AS MEDICAL SUPPLIES.

I'LL WRITE AGAIN SOON AND TILL THEN MY LOVE TO YOU ALL.

YOUR LOVING SON.
LEN

Letter 6

Rangoon 07.09.1945

DEAR MOTHER

HAD A GLORIOUS REUNION YESTERDAY. BOB WHITE, KEN WOLFE, JOHNNIE GLANCY AND THE CRANMER BROTHERS WERE ALL IN THE SAME HOSPITAL, AS WELL AS MANY MORE OF THE REGIMENT. IT WAS GREAT SEEING THEM BECAUSE I HAVE BEEN ON MY OWN FOR MONTHS NOW.

WE SAW A FILM LAST NIGHT CALLED 'HOLLYWOOD CANTEEN', A GREAT SHOW WITH A GREAT CAST. THE SONGS WERE VERY GOOD. NOT HAVING HEARD ANY OF THE LATEST SONGS SINCE 1941, I AM A LONG WAY BEHIND WITH MY REPERTOIRE, AND SO IF POSSIBLE I WOULD LIKE YOU TO SEND ME ONE OR TWO OF THE MOST RECENT SONG HITS.

YOU KNOW THE TYPE I LIKE FROM THE FILMS. IRENE, JEN AND ENA WILL HELP YOU TO CHOOSE THEM; JUST ONE OR TWO SO I CAN CATCH UP. PROBABLY YOU WILL HAVE SOME WHICH YOU BOUGHT FOR THE GIRLS TO LEARN AND IF THEY HAVE LEARNED THEM, YOU CAN SEND THEM AND I WILL BRING THEM WITH ME WHEN I RETURN. I HOPE I AM NOT ASKING TOO MUCH, BUT YOU KNOW MUSIC IS MY WEAK POINT.

YOU MAY OR MAY NOT RECEIVE CONTACT FROM A CAPTAIN DAVID N FFOLKES OF STOURBRIDGE, OR MAYBE HIS MOTHER. HE IS AN OFFICER WHO LOOKED AFTER ME IN ONE OF THE CAMPS AND LARGELY TO HIM I OWE MY LIFE.

HE IS VERY HIGH UP IN THE THEATRE WORLD AS A STAGE DESIGNER. HE HAS WORKED AT THE OLD VIC AND WITH IVOR NOVELLO, BUT MOSTLY IN LONDON AND NEW YORK WITH SHAKESPEARE PLAYS. THE OFFICERS WERE SEPARATED FROM US FIVE MONTHS AGO AND UP TILL THEN, HE HAD LOOKED AFTER ME AS REGARDS EXTRA FOOD AND MONEY, AND AS YOU KNOW THE FOOD WE RECEIVED FROM THE NIPS WAS INADEQUATE. SINCE THEN I LOST CONTACT WITH HIM.

WE ARE STILL BEING WELL LOOKED AFTER AND IT HELPS US NOT TO BE IMPATIENT DURING THE WAITING PERIOD BEFORE REACHING HOME.

LOVE TO IRENE, JENNIE AND ENA AND DAD. I DON'T THINK IT WILL BE LONG BEFORE WE ARE ON THE BOAT COMING HOME. WE ARE BEING TREATED WITH MEPACRINE AND VITAMIN B, SO WE WILL BE AS STRONG AS HORSES IN NO TIME.

CHEERIO AND LOVE TO ALL.

YOUR LOVING SON
LEN

Letter 7

Rangoon 10.09.1945

DEAR MOTHER

I AM STILL IN THE CONVENT HOSPITAL AND ENJOYING IT IMMENSELY. I HAVE HAD A GOOD LOOK AROUND RANGOON. IT HAS SOME MARVELLOUS PAGODAS, BUT THE CITY IS MORE OR LESS RUINED AS THE RESULT OF RECENT FIGHTING.

PICTURES ARE FREE AND I HAVE SEEN SO FAR, "HOLLYWOOD CANTEEN", CHARLES LAUGHTON IN "SUSPECT" AND ANOTHER BRITISH PICTURE. A FEW MINUTES AGO THERE WAS THE SOUND OF CHEERING AND CLAPPING. AIR MARSHALL SIR KEITH PARKES VISITED THE HOSPITAL AND HAS JUST DELIVERED A SPEECH SAYING THAT A DOZEN SHIPS HAVE ARRIVED AND WITHIN TEN DAYS, TWELVE THOUSAND OF US WILL BE ABOARD THEM.

THE TRIP WILL PROBABLY TAKE A LONG TIME AS THEY INTEND TO FATTEN US UP AND GET US FIT ON THE WAY. WE WILL PROBABLY CALL IN AT INDIA OR SOUTH AFRICA FOR A FEW DAYS' LEAVE IN EACH PLACE AND IT WILL, AS FAR AS WE CAN GATHER BE MORE LIKE A CRUISE.

WE HEAR MANY CONFLICTING REPORTS OF CONDITIONS IN ENGLAND, BUT I WILL WAIT AND SEE. WHATEVER HAPPENS, I DOUBT IF I FEEL LIKE GOING BACK TO BINNS IN A FACTORY AGAIN, NOT AFTER SIX YEARS OF LIFE IN THE OPEN.

TALKING OF OPEN, THE PAST THREE YEARS HAVE BEEN ALL OUT IN THE OPEN: NO SHIRTS; STOCKINGS; BOOTS OR SHOES. WE HAVE NOT EVEN HAD TROUSERS, AND ALL WE WORE (IT MAY SOUND INDECENT BUT THE JAPS WOULD NOT GIVE US ANYTHING ELSE) WAS A PIECE OF BLACK CLOTH ABOUT TWO FEET BY NINE INCHES AND A PIECE OF TAPE AROUND THE WAIST. I DON'T KNOW IF YOU CAN VISUALIZE WHAT WE LOOKED LIKE, BUT WE WENT ALL NATIVE AND LOOKED JUST LIKE JUNGLE MEN.

SOME OF THE NATIVES WITH WHOM WE BECAME FRIENDLY WERE HALF WILD MEN. THEY HAD NEVER BEEN OUT OF THE JUNGLE, CARRIED LONG KNIVES AND LIVED ON THE VEGETABLES AND GAME. THEY WERE VERY HELPFUL AT TIMES AS THEY EXTRACTED NEWS FROM THE NATIVES PASSING THROUGH AND PASSED IT ONTO US.

I HAVE SEEN OR HEARD MOST OF THE FELLOWS I KNEW QUITE WELL. I TOLD YOU I'VE SEEN KEN WOLFE, BOB WHITE AND JACK BALDRIDGE, AND I'VE HEARD THAT HAROLD BELL IS IN A CAMP ABOUT TEN MILES AWAY. I HAVE NOT SO FAR BEEN ABLE TO TRACE ERNIE MAUGHAN AND I THINK HE MUST HAVE LEFT THAILAND A WHILE AGO.

I HOPE BY NOW WILF'S MOTHER HAS GOT OVER THE SHOCK OF HIS DEATH. CAPTAIN WATTS AND I WERE AT HIS BEDSIDE WHEN HE DIED. WATTS TOLD ME NOT TO TAKE IT TOO HARD AS WE HAD A LOT TO GO THROUGH BEFORE WE WERE FREE AND MANY MORE OF US WOULD GO THE SAME WAY AS WILF. HE WAS RIGHT; HE DIED HIMSELF A YEAR LATER.

SO YOU SEE, I LOST TWO OF MY BEST FRIENDS EARLY ON AND SO I BECAME A LONE WOLF, AS IT WAS BAD MAKING FRIENDS; MEN WERE DYING SO QUICKLY. DOUG HERBERT DIED FIRST THEN WILF. I THINK IT IS DUE TO YOUR PRAYERS THAT GOD HAS LOOKED AFTER ME AND KEPT ME SAFE.

I HAVE HAD MANY NARROW ESCAPES, AND YOU MAY NOT BELIEVE IT BUT ALL OUR FELLOWS WERE SURPRISED TO SEE ME AS IT WAS REPORTED UNOFFICIALLY THAT I WAS DEAD. I TOLD THEM THAT I MADE A POOR CORPSE AND WE LAUGHED IT OFF: THEY WERE GLAD TO SEE ME SO FIT.

WELL, I HAVE RAMBLED ON AND NOW I AM NEAR TO THE END OF MY PAPER. MY LOVE TO DAD AND SISTERS. I DON'T THINK WE HAVE ANY STABLE ADDRESSES FOR YOU TO WRITE TO, SO I'LL ONLY HAVE TO WAIT FOR A WORD FROM YOU.

(18 MONTHS SINCE I HAD WORD FROM YOU, BUT THAT IS NOT YOUR FAULT.)

I KNOW YOU WERE WRITING EVERY SUNDAY.

BEST OF LUCK TO DAD, SISTERS AND ALL.

YOUR LOVING SON.
LEN

STOP PRESS NEWS

IN OTHER WORDS, I HAVE MORE TO ADD TO WHAT I HAVE ALREADY SAID. THIS WON'T COST YOU A PENNY EXTRA LIKE SAMMY STOREY'S ECHO, BIT IT IS JUST TO SAY THAT, SPEAKING OF HAROLD BELL, HE AND NORMAN JEFFERSON CAME TO SEE ME FROM A CAMP SIX MILES AWAY.

THEY BOTH LOOK FINE AND HAROLD BELL IS ACTUALLY FAT. HAROLD SAYS HE HAS HAD A LETTER FROM YOU, AND NORMAN PASSED ON THE NEWS TO HIS WIFE IRENE. I GOT MY DISCHARGE FROM HOSPITAL AND HAVE BEEN DRAWING MY KIT READY TO LEAVE TOMORROW FOR THE TRANSIT S CAMP.

WE ARE NOW ALL IN GREEN: GREEN SHIRTS, SLACKS AND BERETS. I HAVE BEEN PRACTISING PUTTING MY BERET ON ALL THIS AFTERNOON; IN FACT, THE SISTER WHO LIVES IN BERWICK CAME OUT AND PUT IT INTO SHAPE. THIS SISTER IS A FINE WOMAN AND HAS LOOKED AFTER ME WELL.

AND SO DEAR MOTHER, I MUST BID YOU, "HASTA LA VISTA," FOR THE SECOND TIME. MY NEXT LETTER WILL BE FROM ANOTHER CAMP. IT FEELS FUNNY TO WEAR SHIRTS AGAIN AND BOOTS; I FEEL AS THOUGH MY FEET ARE TWICE THEIR SIZE. STILL IT WON'T TAKE LONG. YOU KNOW MOTHER, I AM EVEN LEARNING TO SCRIBBLE THE WAY I USED TO.

SO CHEERIO EVERYBODY.

LOTS OF LOVE TO ALL. GOD BLESS YOU MOTHER.

LOVING SON.
LEN

Letter 8

At Sea 25.09.1945

DEAR MOTHER

IT IS NOW OVER A WEEK SINCE WE LEFT RANGOON BY BOAT. SO, THAT MEANS WE'VE DONE ABOUT A THIRD OF THE JOURNEY. WE CALLED IN AT PORT A FEW DAYS AGO AND HAD A TREMENDOUS RECEPTION.

INDIAN, HIGHLAND AND MARINE BANDS WERE PLAYING ON THE JETTY AS WE PULLED IN AND WE WERE GUESTS OF THE RED CROSS TO A FIRST-CLASS LUNCH. EVERYONE WAS ABSOLUTELY FINE. WE WERE ONLY ASHORE FOR ABOUT THREE HOURS, BUT WE ENJOYED EVERY MINUTE OF IT.

WRENS AND WAAFS WERE OUR GUIDES AND IT EMBARRASSED US BECAUSE THEY TREATED US LIKE CHILDREN. THEY WERE CARRYING KIT BAGS; HELPING US ON AND OFF THE TRUCKS; GIVING US SEATS AND STANDING THEMSELVES, AND THEY WERE SO STUBBORN THAT WE JUST COULD NOT DO ANYTHING ABOUT IT.

THEY WAITED ON US HAND AND FOOT AND WERE PUTTING US AT EASE AND MAKING A FINE JOB OF IT. THE NAVY ABOARD THEIR VESSELS GAVE A TREMENDOUS CHEER AS WE CAME IN, AND WHEN WE WERE LEAVING ALL THE SHIPS IN THE HARBOUR WERE HOOTING VICTORY V'S; SIGNALLING V'S ON THEIR LIGHTS, AND MINGLED WITH THE CHEERS FROM DIFFERENT SHIPS. IT WAS A FINE DISPLAY AND THE SPIRIT SHOWN BROUGHT LUMPS TO OUR THROATS.

AND NOW WE ARE RACING ONTO OUR NEXT PORT OF CALL. WE ARE NOW BEING PAID IN ENGLISH MONEY AND IT LOOKED VERY STRANGE WHEN WE FIRST HANDLED IT.

LOVE TO ALL AND IT WON'T BE LONG BEFORE WE FOLLOW THIS LETTER.,

DAD, IRENE, JENNIE, ENA AND ALL.

LOVING SON.
LEN

Telegrams:

Rangoon 09.09.1945

ARRIVED SAFELY AT INDIA.

HOPE TO BE HOME SOON.

ADDRESS LETTERS AND TELEGRAMS TO C.O.
RECOVERED F W MAIL CENTRE.

BOMBAY INDIA COMMAND.

OCTOBER
HAVE ARRIVED SAFELY IN THE MIDDLE EAST.

HOPE TO BE HOME SOON. ALL MY LOVE.

TRANSIT CAMP, POVERTY LANE, MAGHULL, LIVERPOOL.

ARRIVED SAFELY, SEE YOU SOON.

EPILOGUE

Released Prisoners of War Photographed at Singapore

Front Row: Left to right
         J A Hood
701716   L A C Kidson, Lyndhurst, Stocksfield on Tyne
7906665 Tpr R Connor, 14 Haig Crescent, Sherburn, Durham
035706   L.bdr E. Hatterton, 2105 Station Road, Wallsend on Tyne

Standing: Left to right
912485   Gnr P Williams, 2 Park Road, Sunderland
994720   Lac W R Watson, Gateshead on Tyne
10084456 Lac W Adamson, Ashington. Northumberland.

Notable Dates

Year	Date	Event
1939	18 May	*Enlisted in TA 2nd 74th Field Regiment*
	26 August	*TA Camp at Whitby*
	1 September	*Mobilised 125 Field Regiment RA*
	3 September	*War Declared*
	December	*Signal Course at Darlington*
1940	February	*Signal Instructor Course. Messines Lines Catterick*
	June	*Moved to Norfolk*
	December	*Moved to Scotland*
1941	March	*Embarked from Gourock in Strathaird – ten days - then disembarked.* *Fire watching in Glasgow, to Stockport,* *Fire watching in Liverpool.* *To Trawsfynnd for firing practice.*
	28 October	*At Avonmouth, embarked on the 'Oronsay'*
	8 November	*Reached Halifax, Nova Scotia*
	9 November	*Transferred to American ships*
	10 November	*Sailed South*
	23 November	*Crossed the Equator*
	7 December	*Pearl Harbour*
	9 December	*Cape Town*
	13 December	*Set sail. Christmas Day in Indian Ocean.* *New Year's Eve in Bombay*
1942	1 January	*By train to Ahmednagar*
	23 January	*Embarked from Bombay in Empress of Asia*
	4 February	*Bombed by Japanese Aircraft*
	5 February	*Attacked by Japs and set alight. Abandoned ship.*
	5 – 15 February	*Battle stations on Singapore*
	15 February	*Singapore capitulation*
	16 February	*Trek to Changi*
	3 April	*Good Friday – trek to River Valley*
	14 October	*Left Singapore by train*
	19 October	*Arrived at Bang Pong*
	21 October	*Left Bang Pong*
	23 October	*Left 14 Rest Stage*
	24 October	*Arrived at Raja*
	25 October	*Arrived at Tardan*
	26 October	*Arrived at Tarsoa*
	17 November	*Left by river for Wampo*
	18 November	*Arrived at Wampo*

Notable Dates *(continued)*

Year	Date	Event
1943	27 April	*Left Wampo for Tarsoa*
	1 May	*Left Tarsoa for South Tonchan*
	23 July	*Left South Tonchan for Tonchan*
	18 August	*By train to Tarsoa*
1944	20 April	*Left Tarsoa by train*
	21 April	*Arrived Non Plladuct*
	23 April	*Arrived Nakon Pathom*
1945	12 April	*Left Nakon Pathom for Kirrikan*
	13 April	*Arrived Kirrikan*
	14 April	*Minoa*
	15 April	*Tagaree*
	16 April	*Border Camp*
	25 May	*Back to Tagaree*
	18 August	*Told war is finished. Moved to Minoa*
	19 August	*To Eakin*
	5 September	*Flew to Rangoon*
	11 September	*5 FAHRU*

Army medic Bill's admiration
for surgeon 'Weary' Dunlop

BILL BROWN remembers well the first Sunderland voice he heard in a PoW camp.

Bill had been in a reserved occupation as an asphalter and wasn't called up until 1941, when he joined the 135 Regiment at Peterborough and was drafted to the Far East where they were taken prisoner.

He was helping in a camp hospital when an appendicitis case came in. The operation was being carried out without anaesthetic and with home-made instruments.

The man was Lenny Gibson, then of Milburn Street, Millfield.

"He was in a bad way at the time, and I said: 'Never mind, lad, when we get home we'll catch the same tram home from the north end of the station.' I lived in the next street, Ravensworth Street, at the time," said Bill, 82, who now lives in Hall Farm Road.

Emotion isn't far away when Bill talks of the condition of some of the prisoners he saw.

And he is still full of admiration for the surgeon he worked with – Edward "Weary" Dunlop, who died in Australia recently. Weary? Dunlop = tyres = tired = weary.

He used to pass instructions down the line to doctors who weren't surgeons. After the war Weary Dunlop was knighted.

MEDIC: Bill Brown, an asphalter before the war, needed a strong stomach to hold down patients being operated on without anaesthetic in PoW camps.

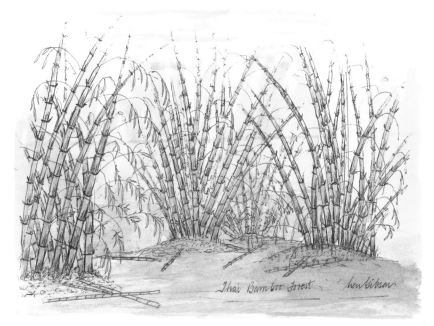

Thai Bamboo Forest   Len Gibson

143